REVIE

"An attitude of gratitude is a must for all who aspire to be champions. Here is an exquisite illustration of the efficacy of exhibiting gratitude, and it is touching. Evangeline makes a compelling case for all children to express gratitude to God for their mothers. She is not just sharing her mother's unprecedented wisdom with us; she is honoring a woman of exceptional grit. This is a must read for all sons and daughters." - Dr. Eric Tangumonkem.

"I never knew Mama Philomena Mbuh Asafor in life, but I wish I had been privy to her godly wisdom back when I was raising my children. In living out the doctrines that shaped her family life, this incredible woman was at the same time as hard as steel and as gentle as a sweet magnolia. What a beautiful world we would live in were everyone to have a mama like her." --Terry Bailey

Dear Krystle,
        Happy Mother's Day! May
Jehovah God use my sweet Mother's
legacy to Bless you and yours.
                                        Eva

MY SWEET MOTHER'S DOCTRINES OF GRATITUDE AND HER FINAL REST WITH JEHOVAH GOD

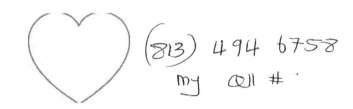

(813) 494 6758
my cell #

BY EVANGELINE N. ASAFOR

ISBN-10: 1-947662-10-4
ISBN-13: 978-1-947662-10-0

Library of Congress Catalog Card Number: 2018909222

DEDICATION

This inspiring piece is dedicated to my sweet mother, Mama Philomena Mbuh Asafor, who was called to be with Jehovah God on the first day of January, 2015. She preached and lived a godly life of gratitude. My sweet mother taught us that striving for excellence in everything we do should be a habit and not an act. Though she only went as far as completing elementary school, this did not keep her from furthering her education. She informally trained herself to become one of the wisest women and teachers who ever lived. She taught by example using practical wisdom, which she shared so generously. She succeeded in raising successful, grateful children who themselves raised successful, grateful children. May my sweet mother's soul continue to rest in peace. Amen!

TABLE OF CONTENTS

Introduction

About My Sweet Mother, Mama Philomena Mbuh Asafor

My sweet mother, Mama Philomena Mbuh Asafor, was born into this world in the early 1930s to Mama Angela Akor, a princess from Kom village, and Papa Atanga, a native of Akum village. She was the middle child of a family of five. She had two older brothers and two younger sisters. She got married in the mid-1950s to Papa Joseph Nkwenti Asafor, a school teacher and philanthropist. Papa Joseph Nkwenti Asafor held a voluntary position as president of the village welfare association for ten years. He will always be remembered by many who were blessed to cross paths with him as a man of integrity and wisdom. His wisdom he shared so generously, and his dedication and guidance gave so many people the wings to fly. He showered my sweet mother with the love she needed, and my sweet mother in return showered him with the respect he deserved.

My sweet mother was the problem solver of the family. She did not go to people for solutions; she always looked to

1

Jehovah God, her Creator, for problem-solving tips. She had no reservations about being second-in-command in the Asafor household because she knew exactly what her role in the family was. Just like Ruth in the Bible, my sweet mother knew that who she was, was different from what she did. She knew her identity and what Jehovah God expected from her. My sweet mother's life on earth was shaped by her faith in Jehovah God, a faith so strong. She shared so generously and so often that it became a way of life amongst her children.

My sweet mother embraced business and farming to support her husband and spent most of her time nurturing and raising her children. She was a very good time manager and raised us under many doctrines, especially doctrines of gratitude. She was the perfect family doctor though without a medical degree.

Rachel Martin's description of a real mother is the perfect definition of my sweet mother. My sweet mother was emotional yet a rock. Even when she was tired, she kept going—sometimes worried but always full of hope. Quitting was never an option even when she was overwhelmed. She was wonderful and amazing even in chaos. She was a life changer right up until she took her last breath and went to be with Jehovah God.

She was a mother to eight kids, twenty-seven grandkids, and nine great-grandchildren. She also left behind one sister,

Mummy Julia, and multiple nieces, nephews, friends, and well-wishers.

After my father was called to be with Jehovah God in 1988, my sweet mother assumed the roles of father and mother to her eight kids, becoming stricter and suddenly developing an extra set of eyes! We could hardly get away with anything. Her sight became magnified, her hearing magical, and her strength almost tripled. The mere sound of her voice scared the truth out of me faster than anything else. In my young eyes, Sweet Mother simply became a magician after my father passed. She could treat any symptom with a prayer and a simple combination of leaves boiled in water, which a sick child would either drink, inhale, or bathe in—sometimes all three. It always worked.

My sweet mother raised us to be resilient and purposeful in whatever we do. I remember as a little girl, I will come up to her in the middle of a task and tell her I was tired, and her response was always " then hurry up and finish what you are doing." This response always instantly fueled me up to complete the task in question. Consequently, I grew up with the notion that you don't stop doing what you're doing because you're tired, you stop when you have finished doing what you started. She was blessed with a gift of discernment and this was consistently manifested in her heightened awareness of God's presence and anointing and an ability to see behind what others say and present.

I watched Sweet Mother live a life of loving, forgiving, and offering the best of who she was, not only to her children and extended family but to others as well. Her life of gratitude taught me to live, love, and learn, and to offer the best of who I am no matter how difficult the situation. I can never thank Jehovah God enough for placing me in the womb of a woman so wonderful, a special woman who became my sweet mother.

My sweet mother lived her life here on earth in accordance with the Holy Spirit. She lived a life of love, joy, peace, patience, kindness, goodness, faithfulness, gentleness, and self-control (Galatians 5:22–23). I hope and pray that *My Sweet Mother's Doctrines of Gratitude* will help readers to live a life of gratitude in accordance with the Holy Spirit.

The following are among the many doctrines my sweet mother embraced and raised her children to embrace:

1. **Show Gratitude to Jehovah God by Accepting Jesus Christ as Your Lord and Savior**

2. **Thanksgiving First Thing in the Morning**

3. **When You Give, Don't Remember; When You Receive, Never Forget**

4. **Show Gratitude When Visiting in Someone's House**

5. **Gratitude is Better Lived than Preached**

6. Gratitude is a Game Changer

7. Gratitude is a Duty of a Lifetime

8. There is a Consequence for Ingratitude

9. Always Remember What Jehovah God Has Already Done in Your Life

10. Show Gratitude by Respecting Those Whom Jehovah God Has Placed in Authority Over You

11. Show Gratitude to Jehovah God by Forgiving Others

12. Show Gratitude to Jehovah God by Reaching Out to Those in Need

13. Show Gratitude to Jehovah God by Including All Things in Your Gratitude

14. Don't Take Life for Granted; Take Life with Gratitude

15. Show Gratitude to Jehovah God by Choosing Your Friends Wisely

16. Show Gratitude to Jehovah God by Using Your Time on Earth Wisely

17. Show Gratitude to Jehovah God by Loving and Accepting Yourself

18. Show Gratitude to Jehovah God by Loving Your Neighbor as Yourself

Chapter 1

First Doctrine of Gratitude: Show Gratitude to Jehovah God by Accepting Jesus Christ as Your Lord and Savior

My sweet mother accepted Jesus Christ as her Lord and Savior as a little girl. She was baptized, received Holy Communion, received confirmation, and got married in the church, when she found her soulmate. Christ was always at the center of her life, and she raised her children with the belief that we needed to accept Jesus Christ as our Lord and Savior to be saved and to enter the kingdom of God. She reiterated that accepting Jesus Christ as Lord and Savior was a terrific way of showing our gratitude to Jehovah God.

What the Bible Says about Accepting Jesus Christ as Your Lord and Savior:

1. *Acts 2:38.* "Then Peter said unto them, 'Repent, and be baptized every one of you in the name of Jesus

Christ for the remission of sins, and ye shall receive the gift of the Holy Ghost.'"

2. *Acts 16:31.* "And they said, 'Believe on the Lord Jesus Christ, and thou shalt be saved, and thy house.'"

3. *Acts 2:21.* "And it shall come to pass, [that] whosoever shall call on the name of the Lord shall be saved."

4. *Galatians 3:26.* "For ye are all the children of God by faith in Christ Jesus."

5. *John 1:12.* "Yet to all who did receive him, to those who believed in his name, he gave the right to become children of God."

6. *1 John 1:6–9.* "If we claim to have fellowship with him and yet walk in the darkness, we lie and do not live out the truth. But if we walk in the light, as he is in the light, we have fellowship with one another, and the blood of Jesus, his Son, purifies us from all sin. If we claim to be without sin, we deceive ourselves and the truth is not in us. If we confess our sins, he is faithful and just and will forgive us our sins and purify us from all unrighteousness."

7. *John 3:16.* "For God so loved the world that he gave his one and only Son, that whoever believes in him shall not perish but have eternal life."

8. *Mark 16:16.* "Whoever believes and is baptized will be saved, but whoever does not believe will be condemned."

9. *Revelation 3:20.* "Here I am! I stand at the door and knock. If anyone hears my voice and opens the door, I will come in and eat with that person, and they with me."

10. *Romans 10:9–10.* "If you declare with your mouth, 'Jesus is LORD,' and believe in your heart that God raised him from the dead, you will be saved. For it is with your heart that you believe and are justified, and it is with your mouth that you profess your faith and are saved."

11. *Romans 6:23.* "For the wages of sin is death, but the gift of God is eternal life in Christ Jesus our LORD."

12. *1 Thessalonians 5:23.* "May God himself, the God of peace, sanctify you through and through. May your whole spirit, soul and body be kept blameless at the coming of our LORD Jesus Christ."

Chapter 2

Second Doctrine of Gratitude: Thanksgiving First Thing in the Morning

Growing up in Akum village with my sweet mother and the rest of my siblings was very interesting and colored with memories that we all cherish. My sweet mother believed, preached, and practiced waking up every morning and beginning the day on her knees in thanksgiving. She taught us to always start the day by rising and praising God for another day and for his goodness and mercies. Just like Roy T. Bennett once said, "Gratitude begins when you wake up in the morning and start each day with a positive thought and a grateful heart."

I remember hearing my sweet mother always singing this song: "In the morning, early in the morning, in the morning, I will rise and praise the Lord." This song comes to my mind very often when I open my eyes first thing in the morning and even when I work overnight and get off work in the morning. My sweet mother always reminded me that if I don't remember to ask Jehovah God for directions first thing in the morning, every morning, I will surely get lost in life's many twists and turns. With an attitude of gratitude, I watched my sweet mother start her day with prayer and end her day with prayer. She had an unlimited list of things to thank Jehovah God for every day, and it did not matter what circumstances we were in. My sweet mother always looked up to the heavens with faith that prayers going up would bring blessings down. My sweet mother believed, and nurtured us to believe, that the most appropriate time to meet Jehovah God and to fellowship with Him is early in the morning. After all, she reiterated, manna is gathered before the sun rises (Exodus 16:14-21), so those who want to partake in the spiritual nourishment of Jehovah God must plan on getting in the gratitude and fellowship mood early in the morning.

What the Bible Says About Praying First Thing in the Morning:

1. *Genesis 19:27.* "Now Abraham arose early in the morning and went to the place where he had stood before the Lord."

2. *1 Chronicles 23:30.* "They are to stand every morning to praise and thank Jehovah God, and likewise at evening."

3. *Isaiah 33:2.* "Lord, be gracious to us; we long for you. Be our strength every morning, our salvation in time of distress."

4. *Job 38*:12. "Have you commanded the morning since your days began and caused the dawn to know its place?"

5. *Mark 1:35.* "And rising very early in the morning while it was still dark, he departed and went out to a desolate place, and there he prayed."

6. *Psalm 90:14.* "Satisfy us in the morning with your steadfast love, that we may rejoice and be glad all our days."

7. *Psalm 5*:3. "O Lord, in the morning you hear my voice, in the morning I will order my prayer to you and eagerly watch."

8. *Psalm 59:16.* "But I will sing of your strength, I will sing aloud of your steadfast love in the morning. For you have been to me a fortress and a refuge in the day of my distress."

9. *Psalm 143:8.* "Let the morning bring me word of your unfailing love, for I have put my trust in you. Show me the way I should go, for to you I entrust my life."

10. *Psalm 119:147.* "I rise before dawn and cry for help; I wait for your words."

11. *1 Samuel 1:19.* "Then they arose early in the morning and worshipped before the Lord."

What the Bible Says About Jehovah God's Servants Who Dealt with Him in the Morning:

1. *Abraham—Genesis 22:3.* "Early the next morning Abraham got up and loaded his donkey. He took with him two of his servants and his son Isaac. When he had cut enough wood for the burnt offering, he set out for the place God had told him about.

2. *David—1 Samuel 17:20.* "And David rose up early in the morning and left the sheep with a keeper, and took and went as Jesse had commanded him."

3. *Hannah—1 Samuel 1:19.* "Early the next morning they arose and worshiped before the LORD and then went back to their home at Ramah."

4. *Job—Job 1:5.* "When a period of feasting had run its course, Job would plan for them to be purified. Early in the morning he would sacrifice a burnt offering for each of them, thinking, 'Perhaps my children have sinned and cursed God in their hearts.' This was Job's regular custom."

5. *Jacob—Genesis 28:18.* "Early the next morning Jacob took the stone he had placed under his head and set it up as a pillar and poured oil on top of it."

6. *Joshua—Joshua 6:12.* "Joshua got up early the next morning and the priests took up the ark of the LORD."

7. *Mary—Luke 24:22.* "In addition, some of our women amazed us. They went to the tomb early this morning." *John 20:1.* "Early on the first day of the week, while it was still dark, Mary Magdalene went to the tomb and saw that the stone had been removed from the entrance."

8. *Moses—Exodus 8:20.* "Then the LORD said to Moses, 'Get up early in the morning and confront Pharaoh as he goes to the river and say to him, "This is what the LORD says: Let my people go, so that they may worship me."'"

9. *The apostles—Acts 5:21.* "At daybreak they entered the temple courts, as they had been told, and began to teach the people. When the high priest and his associates arrived, they called together the Sanhedrin—the full assembly of the elders of Israel—and sent to the jail for the apostles."

What Some Great Minds Say About Praying to Jehovah God as a Sign of Gratitude:

1. *Abraham Lincoln.* "I know that the Lord is always on the side of the right; but it is my constant anxiety and prayer that I and this nation may be on the Lord's side." "I have been driven many times upon my knees by the overwhelming conviction that I had nowhere else to go. My own wisdom and that of all about me seemed insufficient for that day."

2. *Adrian Rogers.* "The prayer offered to God in the morning during your quiet time is the key that unlocks the door of the day. Any athlete knows that it is the start that ensures a good finish."

3. *Billy Graham.* "The Christian life is not a constant high. I have my moments of deep discouragement. I must go to God in prayer with tears in my eyes, and say, 'O God, forgive me,' or 'Help me.'" "To get nations back on their feet, we must first get down on our knees."

4. *Charles Spurgeon.* "If you believe in prayer at all, expect God to hear you. If you do not expect, you will not have. God will not hear you unless you believe He will hear you; but if you believe He will, He will be as good as your faith."

5. *Joyce Meyer.* "Prayer is simply talking to God like a friend and should be the easiest thing we do each day."

6. *Mother Teresa.* "God shapes the world by prayer. The more praying there is in the world the better the world will be, the mightier the forces against evil." "God speaks in the silence of the heart. Listening is the beginning of prayer."

7. *Thomas Kinkade.* "Rather than set aside daily time for prayer, I pray constantly and spontaneously about everything I encounter on a daily basis. When someone shares something with me, I'll often simply say, 'Let's pray about this right now.'"

Chapter 3

Third Doctrine of Gratitude: When You Give, Don't Remember; When You Receive, Never Forget

Growing up around my sweet mother, she constantly told us about people who had helped her in the past. I heard these stories so much that I started getting fed up. One time while I was in my teenage years, we were going to the farm, which was a good eight-mile walk, and about six miles into the walk, my sweet mother brought up a story about this lady who once helped her. This was about the hundredth time I was listening to this story. Tired and frustrated, I gathered the courage to ask her why we had to go through the torture of listening to stories of people, most of whom were dead or otherwise unknown to us. As if that question was not daring enough, I asked my sweet mother if she did not have any stories about the things she did for others. She stopped, held me on my shoulders, and said, "My daughter, always remember this: when you give, don't remember, and when you receive, never forget." Finally, I got it—though I would still continue listening to these stories for the rest of my life. Sweet Mother made sure stories of gratitude were told at the fireside, while going to the farm, while doing farm work, and while coming home from a long day of farming. Whenever we did something good for someone and wanted to sing our own praises, my sweet mother would tell us she was proud of us but should never hear that story again.

When my sweet mother was with me in America, I got my tithing records in the mail from my church, and I told her that the good thing about tithing is that you get to report what you offered as a tithe when you file a tax return and most often get the money back. She shook her head, looked at me, and said, "America really is the headquarters of the devil. Why would any right-thinking Christian want to know how much they have offered to Jehovah God, let alone try to use that amount to get a tax break?" I looked at her confused and answered, "Sweet Mother, that's the way it's done in America." She laughed and said, "My daughter, there is a lot of good in America and plenty of bad; embrace only the good things. Throw that tithing record in the trash." It dawned on me then that I was not fully practicing her doctrine of gratitude, the one about not remembering when you give. From that time on, I never looked at my tithing record again nor dared to use it for filing taxes.

In 2007, my husband was arrested for immigration irregularities, leaving me with four children to care for alone. So many people offered us prayers, financial support, time, and food. Having this doctrine of gratitude engrained in me and fearing that I might forget some of the people who were calling or stopping by, I got a notebook and wrote down what I received from each person so I could later thank God for them. In doing this, I had a powerful encounter with God that prompted the writing of my inspirational book, *My Prayers of Gratitude to Jehovah God.* In the midst of this trial, with my husband locked up and my hands full caring for four kids plus working, I always met God on the pages of my notebook. It was where I told Jehovah God exactly what was going on and thanked him for it all. Throughout my ordeal, I never forgot to thank Jehovah God for everyone who helped me, and I never forgot what each one did to move me from one stage to another. Thanks to my sweet mother's doctrine of gratitude, I was able to remember, pray, and thank Jehovah God for every blessing I received. This doctrine of gratitude is one of my special tools for a rewarding spiritual life, and I am making sure I share it generously with my children and the rest of humanity.

What the Bible Says About Never Forgetting What You Receive from Jehovah God:

1. *I Chronicles 16:12.* "Remember the wonderful deeds Jehovah God has done, his marvels, and the judgements from his mouth."

2. *Deuteronomy 5:15.* "You shall remember that you were a slave in the land of Egypt, I and Jehovah God brought you out of there by a mighty hand and by an outstretched arm; therefore, the Lord your God commanded you to show gratitude by observing the Sabbath day."

3. *Deuteronomy 4:10.* "We should always remember what Jehovah God has already done for us, to give us hope that he will do what he has promised."

4. *Hebrews 10:32–35 (NIV).* "Remember those earlier days after you had received the light, when you endured in a great conflict full of suffering. Sometimes you were publicly exposed to insult and persecution; at other times you stood side by side with those who were so treated. You suffered along with those in prison and joyfully accepted the confiscation of your property, because you knew that you yourselves had better and lasting possessions. So, do not throw away your confidence; it will be richly rewarded by Jehovah God."

5. *John 14:15.* Genuine love for Jehovah God is stimulated by remembering what he has done for us in Christ Jesus.

6. *Matthew 25:36:* "Naked, and you clothed me, I was sick, and you visited me, I was in prison, and you came to me."

7. *Revelation 3:3 (NASB)*. "So remember what you have received and heard; and keep it, and repent therefore if you do not wake up, I will come like a thief, and you will not know at what hour I will come to you."

Chapter 4
Fourth Doctrine of Gratitude: Show Gratitude When Visiting in Someone's House

Sometimes when my sweet mother would visit my sisters or brothers in Yaounde, I was fortunate to be around. I noticed she had the habit of taking a shower first thing in the morning before other people in the house got up. When I had my first daughter in Yaounde and my sweet mother spent one year with me in my Biyemassi apartment, she would shower before any of us got up. When she spent five years with me in America, she would shower before anyone got up. It was rare to see my mother getting a shower while people were up and about. A month before her passing, she was living with my brother in Yaounde, and I flew home to see her. I shared her bed with her, and after taking a bath first thing in the morning, she would get me up to go take a bath too before my brother and his wife got up. I reluctantly obeyed but decided to find out the whole doctrine behind this bathing before people got up. After oiling my back for me on the second day of taking early showers, I dressed, sat on the bed next to her, and asked her what the early shower was all about. She looked at me, told me how beautiful I looked, and said, "My sweet daughter, when you are in anyone's house—I mean anyone, it does not matter if it's your child, sister, brother, or a total stranger's house—show them gratitude by not being in their way if they need to use their bathroom." I looked at her surprisingly and said, "Sweet Mother, there are three bathrooms in this house, and Emmanuel told me this one we use is specifically reserved for you." My sweet mother patted me on my back and said, "My sweet daughter, never take anyone's hospitality for granted; take it with gratitude. Being in another person's house is enough inconvenience. Stay out of their way as much as possible." I reluctantly but obediently embraced this doctrine of gratitude, and for the next ten days in Cameroon, I got up early and showered after my sweet mother but before the rest of the family got up.

What the Bible Says about Showing an Attitude of Gratitude When Visiting in Someone's House:

1. *Colossians 3:20.* "Children, obey your parents in everything, for this pleases Jehovah God."

2. *John 13:34–35.* "A new command I give you: Love one another. As I have loved you, so you must love

one another. By this, everyone will know that you are my disciples, if you love one another."

3. *Matthew 7:12.* "So, in everything, do to others what you would have them do to you, for this sums up the Law of the Prophets."

4. *Philippians 2:3.* "Do nothing out of selfish ambition or vain conceit. Rather, in humility value others above yourselves."

5. *1 Peter 2:17.* "Show proper respect to everyone, love the family of believers, fear God, honor the emperor."

6. *Proverbs 1:8.* "Hear, my son, your father's instruction, and forsake not your mother's teaching."

7. *Romans 12:10.* "Love one another with brotherly affection. Outdo one another in showing honor."

8. *Titus 2:7.* "In everything set them an example by doing what is good. In your teaching show integrity, seriousness..."

Chapter 5

Fifth Doctrine of Gratitude: Gratitude Is Better Lived than Preached

My sweet mother, Mama Philomena, lived a life of gratitude and taught her children to do the same. She believed that the best sermons are lived, not preached, and nurtured her children to believe the same and live lives of gratitude. As John F. Kennedy once said, "As we express our gratitude, we must never forget that the highest appreciation is not to utter words but to live by them." My sweet mother gave thanks to God in both good times and bad and lived a life of thanksgiving. Just like Neal A. Maxwell, my sweet mother believed that counting one's blessings was a good thing, but making one's blessings count was even better. My Sweet Mother believed that life was such a precious gift that everyone living had to be thankful for life through their actions and not by words alone.

What the Bible Says About Gratitude Better Lived than Preached:

1. *2 Corinthians 8:2.* In the midst of a very severe trial, the Macedonians' overflowing joy and their extreme poverty welled up in rich generosity. Jehovah God appreciates it when we give out of inner motivation and not outward compulsion. These Macedonian believers gave cheerfully, not begrudgingly or under compulsion.

2. *Jonah 2:9.* "But I, with shouts of grateful praise, will sacrifice to you. What I have vowed I will make good. I will say, 'Salvation comes from the LORD.'"

3. *Mark 12:41–44.* Jesus commended the poor widow who gave all she had to live on, but He was not impressed with the large gifts of the rich, because they had much left over.

4. *Matthew 6:21.* "Where your treasure is, there will your heart be also." Giving reflects the condition of our hearts and speaks of our gratitude to Jehovah God louder than any words imaginable. Living a life of gratitude means intentionally and generously giving to any area of need Jehovah God assigns. You must pray constantly for your assignment and receive it with an attitude of gratitude.

5. *1 Timothy 6:18.* "Command them to do good, to be rich in virtuous deeds, and to be generous and willing to share."

Chapter 6
Sixth Doctrine of Gratitude: Gratitude is a Game Changer

When we were growing up, my sweet mother had zero tolerance for ungratefulness or even hints of it. If you did not say thank you loud enough or soon enough after receiving something, whatever was given to you was taken away. We practiced saying thank you so much that some of my siblings would be heard saying thank you in their sleep! My Sweet Mother always channeled our gratitude to Jehovah God immediately upon receiving anything. As William Arthur Ward once said, "Gratitude can transform common days into thanksgivings, turn routine jobs into joy, and change ordinary opportunities into blessings." As simple as a thank-you may sound, it is a powerful tool for success and godliness in anyone's life who recognizes its importance. A grateful attitude can set anyone free from the prison of disempowerment and the handcuffs of gloom (Steve Maraboli). My sweet mother always expressed her gratitude and encouraged her children to do same. She believed in the expression of gratitude no matter the circumstance, hour, or cost. Just like Steve Maraboli, my sweet mother believed that anyone who cultivates the ability to be grateful equally creates the ability to achieve greatness. Feeling gratitude and not expressing it is like wrapping a gift and not giving it (William Arthur Ward). My sweet mother believed that gratitude was that spice that could change the mundane into the magical and make life become even more pleasant. As Dietrich Bonhoeffer once said, "In ordinary life, we hardly realize that we receive a great deal more than we give and that it is only with gratitude that life becomes rich." My sweet mother believed and preached that if you take things in life with gratitude and not for granted, fear will disappear, and abundance will appear.

What the Bible Says About Gratitude being a Game Changer:

1. *Acts 16:22–40.* Paul and Silas were stripped, beaten, and thrown into prison for teaching about Jesus. Paul and Silas displayed an attitude of gratitude by praying and singing hymns to Jehovah God, suddenly there was an earthquake and all the prison doors were open and the chains fell off the prisoners.

2. *Daniel 6.* King Darius was forced by the law of the land to throw Daniel to the ravenous lions for disrespecting the decree forbidding anyone from making

petitions to "any god or man for thirty days except king Darius." With an attitude of gratitude, Daniel continued to pray and thank Jehovah God, and Jehovah God rescued Daniel by sending his angel to shut the mouths of the lions so they didn't harm Daniel. Jehovah God also severely punished Daniel's adversaries.

3. *James 1:2.* "Blessed is the man who remains steadfast under trial, for when he has stood the test he will receive the crown of life, which Jehovah God has promised to those who love him."

4. *John 16*:33. "I have said these things to you, that in me you may have peace. In the world you will have tribulation, but take heart, I have overcome the world."

5. *Jonah 2:9.* "But I, with shouts of grateful praise, will sacrifice to you. What I have vowed I will make good. I will say, 'Salvation comes from the LORD.'"

6. *Philippians 4:6–7.* When you present your prayer and petition to Jehovah God with an attitude of gratitude, the peace of Jehovah God which transcends all understanding will guard your hearts and minds in Jesus Christ.

7. *1 Thessalonians 5:18.* "Give thanks in all circumstances; for this is God's will for you in Christ Jesus."

Chapter 7
Seventh Doctrine of Gratitude: Gratitude is a Duty of a Lifetime

As a little girl growing up and saying so many thank-yous, I had the audacity one day to ask my sweet mother if I still had to be saying thank you when I grow up and get married. She looked at me with a frown and said, "Gratitude is a life sentence; no way out for you." That said, I had no choice but to accept my verdict and faithfully serve my life sentence of a life of gratitude. My sweet mother never forgot, nor did she let us children forget, those who helped her along the way. She reminded us to lift others up as well. Gratitude was a virtue my sweet mother cherished so much, and as Marcus Tullius Cicero once said, "Gratitude is not only the greatest of virtues, but the parent of all others." My sweet mother believed and preached that to embrace gratitude as a way of life, it must be taught and practiced consistently. As Maya Angelou once said, "Let gratitude be the pillow upon which you kneel to say your nightly prayer."

When I was much younger, my sweet mother had so much to teach and show about gratitude. It took me a while to fully grasp the doctrine that gratitude is a duty, meaning to embrace it as a natural, permanent state, whether we are in a good mood or not. My sweet mother constantly reminded us that gratitude and duty go hand in hand. I was sometimes frustrated when my sweet mother would give thanks to Jehovah God even when one of us would fall on the slippery slopes on the way to or from our farm. But later in life, when I fully understood gratitude as a duty, my sweet mother's attitude and teachings of gratitude as a duty totally and finally made sense to me. It has been a struggle for me to fully embrace gratitude as a natural, permanent state no matter my situation. However, my sweet mother's voice and the awesome presence of Jehovah God in my life have always reminded me to stay focused and to continue to embrace gratitude as a duty. I now acknowledge, share with others, and nurture my children to know that Jehovah God deserves our every thought and breath at all times, anywhere we are, and no matter what we are going through. Gratitude should be a way of life, naturally flowing from our hearts and our mouths and being handed down from generation to generation and brother to brother.

My sweet mother believed and preached that everyone who has breath should start and end the day with a prayer of gratitude regardless of how the day went. Gratitude is perfect medicine for the soul, and if the only prayer one said was "Thank you, Jehovah God," that would be enough (Meister Eckhart).

Gratitude is a duty. Giving and showing thanks in all we do and say is expected of us by Jehovah God and is in no way optional (Luke 17:10). As Jean-Jacques Rousseau once said, "Gratitude is a duty which ought to be paid, but which none have a right to expect."

My sweet mother lived a life of gratitude and raised her children under many doctrines, especially the doctrine of gratitude. Her last breath was used to thank Jehovah God. Gratitude is progressive, never complete until we meet our Maker, Jehovah God.

What the Bible Says About Gratitude Being a Duty of a Lifetime:

1. *1 Chronicles 23:30.* "They are to stand every morning to praise and thank Jehovah God, and likewise at evening."

2. *Colossians 3:17.* "Whatever you do in word or deed, do all in the name of the Lord Jesus giving thanks through him to Jehovah God."

3. *Colossians 3:15.* "Let the peace of Christ rule in your hearts, since as members of one body you were called to peace. And be thankful."

35

4. *Hebrews 6:10.* "For God *is* not unrighteous to for-get your work and labour of love, which ye have shewed toward his name, in that ye have ministered to the saints, and do minister."

5. *Hebrews 12:28.* "Therefore, since we are receiving a kingdom that cannot be shaken, let us be thankful, and so worship God acceptably with reverence and awe"

6. *Jonah 2:9.* "But I, with shouts of grateful praise, will sacrifice to you. What I have vowed I will make good. I will say, 'Salvation comes from the LORD.'"

7. *Philippians 2:14.* "Do all things without grumbling or questioning."

8. *Psalm 55:16–17.* "But I will call on God, and the LORD will rescue me. Morning, noon, and night I cry out in my distress, and the LORD hears my voice."

9. *Romans 12:1–2.* Therefore, I urge you, brothers and sisters, in view of God's mercy, to offer your bodies as a living sacrifice, holy and pleasing to God. This is your true and proper worship. Do not con-form to the pattern of this world but be transformed by the renewing of your mind. Then you will be able to test and approve what God's will is—his good, pleasing and perfect will."

10. *1 Thessalonians 2:13.* "And we also thank God continually because, when you received the word

of God, which you heard from us, you accepted it not as a human word, but as it actually is, the word of God, which is indeed at work in you who believe."

11. *Thessalonians 5:16-18.* "Be joyful always; pray continually; give thanks in all circumstances, for this is Jehovah God's will for you in Christ Jesus."

Chapter 8

Eighth Doctrine of Gratitude: There is a Consequence for Ingratitude

Though my sweet mother consistently preached to us about gratitude and encouraged us to live a life of gratitude, she did not forget to warn us about the dire consequences of ingratitude as mentioned in the Holy Bible. She constantly reminded us that Jehovah God appreciates gratitude and expects it from all his children. Jehovah God hates ingratitude and loves our being thankful in both good and troubled times (Judges 3:7). As Thomas Merton once said, "To be grateful is to recognize the love of God in everything he has given us—and he has given us everything." This harsh reality reinforced in us the desire to be grateful to Jehovah God for everything for fear that just like my sweet mother, he might take away the things he had given us. I remember as a little girl thanking Jehovah God for the air we breathe, the water we drink, and the food we eat, because I knew for a fact that if he took away these three things, we would die. I thanked Jehovah God for heavy rain and even prayed for heavy rain, so we could skip walking eight miles to the farm and stay home by the fireside telling stories and sharing jokes with our parents and siblings. My prayers for heavy rainfall were answered very often during the peak periods of the rainy season. I was truly thankful for those rainy days when it became impossible to go to the farm or to fetch water or firewood.

What the Bible Says About the Consequences of Ingratitude:

1. *Colossians 3:25.* "For the wrongdoer will be paid back for the wrong he has done, and there is no partiality."

2. *Genesis 2:17.* "But from the tree of the knowledge of good and evil you shall not eat, for in the day that you eat from it, you will surely die."

3. *Isaiah 13:11.* "I will punish the world for their evil, and the wicked for their iniquity, and I will cause the arrogance of the proud to cease and will lay low the haughtiness of the terrible."

4. *James 2:10.* "For whoever keeps the whole law but fails in one point has become accountable for all of it."

5. *Proverbs 24:22.* "For their calamity will rise suddenly and who knows the ruin that comes from both?"

6. *Proverbs 2:22.* "But the wicked will be cut off from the land and the treacherous will be uprooted from it."

7. *Revelation 20:15.* "And if anyone's name is not found written in the book of life, he was thrown into the lake of fire."

8. *Romans 1:21.* "For although they knew God, they did not honor him as God or give thanks to him, but they became futile in their thinking and their foolish hearts were darkened."

9. *Timothy 3:2.* "The absence of gratitude will make people lovers of self, lovers of money, proud, arrogant, abusive, disobedient to their parents, unholy, ungrateful."

Chapter 9

Ninth Doctrine of Gratitude: Always Remember What Jehovah God Has Already Done in Your Life

Growing up and seeing our dear father always sick was really traumatizing, especially to us young ones who never fully understood his illness and always prayed to God not to take him. Whenever he fell ill, we cried and hoped for the best, but every time we worried and cried, my sweet mother would remind us that he had gone through worse episodes and Jehovah God had healed him. That assurance helped us to have faith in Jehovah God, trusting him to allow us to keep our dear papa for as long as possible. When we were faced with crises, my sweet mother always reminded us that we had survived worse crises in the past. Because she always remembered what Jehovah God had already done in our lives, we were raised to have faith in him no matter what our circumstances.

My sweet mother was like Job in the Bible, who never forgot the things Jehovah God had done in his life while he was going through trials and tribulations. When Job lost all his children, his servants, his sheep, his oxen, and his camels, his wife advised him to "curse God and die." Instead, Job worshipped Jehovah God and blessed his name. He acknowledged that everything he had was given to him by Jehovah God, who also had the authority to take it away. Job did not lose faith in Jehovah God because he remembered all that Jehovah God had already given him and knew that even though he had taken almost all of it away except his wife, he was also capable of giving him even more. Job's life before his trials was colored with blessings and abundance, and though his wife forgot that, Job never forgot. At the end of Job's trials, Jehovah God recognized his faith, spoke to him, and restored him. Jehovah God blessed Job with twice as much as he had before his trials began.

The story of Job and my sweet mother's doctrine of gratitude conclude that if we will always remember the wonderful things Jehovah God has already done in our lives, we can stay positive and faithful during trials and tribulations. My sweet mother warned that we should always fear the Lord and serve him faithfully with all our hearts and never to forget all the wonderful things he has done for us. Samuel, an adviser to King Saul, addressed the people of Israel exhorting them to walk in the way of the Lord. He told them, "But be sure to fear the Lord and serve him faithfully with all your heart; consider what wonderful things he has done for you" (1 Samuel 12:24-25).

What the Bible Says About Remembering What Jehovah God Has Already Done in Your Life:

1. *1 Chronicles 16:12.* "Remember the wonderful deeds Jehovah God has done, his marvels, and the judgements from his mouth."

2. *Deuteronomy 4:10.* "Remember the day you stood before the LORD your God at Horeb, when he said to me, "Assemble the people before me to hear my words so that they may learn to revere me as long as they live in the land and may teach them to their children."

3. *Deuteronomy 5:15.* "You shall remember that you were a slave in the land of Egypt, I and Jehovah God brought you out of there by a mighty hand and by an outstretched arm; therefore, the Lord your God commanded you to show gratitude by observing the Sabbath day."

4. *Hebrews 10:32–35.* "Remember those earlier days after you had received the light, when you endured in a great conflict full of suffering. Sometimes you were publicly exposed to insult and persecution; at other times you stood side by side with those who were so treated. You suffered along with those in

45

prison and joyfully accepted the confiscation of your property because you knew that you yourselves had better and lasting possessions. So do not throw away your faith. It will be richly rewarded by Jehovah God."

5. *John 14:15.* "If you love me, keep my commands."

6. *Matthew 25:36.* "Naked, and you clothed me, I was sick, and you visited me, I was in prison, and you came to me."

7. *Revelation 3:3.* "Remember, therefore, what you have received and heard; hold it fast, and repent. But if you do not wake up, I will come like a thief, and you will not know at what time I will come to you."

8. *1 Thessalonians 5:18.* "Give thanks in all circumstances; for this is God's will for you in Christ Jesus."

Chapter 10

Tenth Doctrine of Gratitude: Show Gratitude by Respecting Those Whom Jehovah God Has Placed Over You

Respecting those whom Jehovah God has placed over us was a doctrine my sweet mother preached so often that it became our way of life. We practiced this doctrine generously with everyone including our parents, our teachers, the priest, local authorities, elders in the village, neighbors, and our older sisters and brothers, to name a few. Growing up in Akum village, it was our culture to call any sibling who was at least one year older "Ndia," which loosely translated is simply an acknowledgement that Jehovah God has placed that sibling over you. My sweet mother would not tolerate any sibling who would not respect that aspect of our culture, our family values. She was a very obedient wife to my father and showed him great love and respect. My father, on the other hand, cherished her. She gave my father the respect he deserved; he gave her the love she desired.

My sweet mother had an older brother who lived in the village and was very rich, powerful, influential—well respected by many and feared by most. My sweet mother's brother was very stingy towards her. He did not help her financially and would hardly even give her a ride in his car. I did not really like him because I could not understand how he could have so much money and not help his own sibling who was barely making ends meet. I would stubbornly ask my sweet mother why she keeps praying for him, praising him, and taking food to him when we barely had enough to eat. My sweet mother scolded me many times, ignored me so many times, and pushed me away quite a few times, but I was not going to shut up without an explanation. So one day after having enough of me, my sweet mother sat me down and explained to me: "My stubborn child, you may never understand why I love and respect my brother the way I do, but Jehovah God is happy with me. The fact that my brother is rich and powerful makes people in this village respect me, and even though he does not give me money, he always makes time for me whenever I want us to talk about family matters. For that I thank Jehovah God. And just so you know, my brother worked hard for his money and does not owe me or you anything." My sweet mother's explanation left me in tears. I realized that not only was she showing gratitude to Jehovah God by respecting her older brother, but she loved him unconditionally. Respecting those Jehovah God has

48

placed over us pleases him. My Sweet Mother believed that respecting authority begins with submitting oneself to the authority of Jesus Christ as Lord of your life.

What the Bible Says About Showing Gratitude by Respecting Those Whom Jehovah God Has Placed Over You:

1. *Acts 24:3.* "We acknowledge this in every way and everywhere, most excellent Felix, with all thanksgiving."

2. *Acts 28:10.* "They honored us in many ways; and when we were ready to sail, they furnished us with the supplies we needed."

3. *Colossians 3:18–20.* "Wives, submit yourselves to your husbands, as is fitting in the LORD. Husbands, love your wives and do not be harsh with them. Children, obey your parents in everything, for this pleases the LORD."

4. *Ephesians 6:1–4.* "Children, respect and obey your parents in the Lord, for this is right."

5. *Romans 13:1-2.* "Let everyone be subject to the governing authorities, for there is no authority except that which God has established. The authorities that exist have been established by God. Consequently, whoever rebels against the authority is rebelling against what God has instituted, and those who do so will bring judgment on themselves."

What Some Great Minds Say About Respecting Those Whom Jehovah God Has Placed Over You:

1. *Elisabeth Elliot.* "Until the will and the affections are brought under the authority of Christ, we have not begun to understand, let alone to accept, His lordship."

2. *George Washington.* "Government is not mere advice; it is authority, with power to enforce its laws."

3. *Paul David Tripp.* "Rejection of parental authority is a rejection of God's authority. And the rejection of God's authority is, in fact, claiming his authority as my own. It is an attempt to be God."

4. *Robert Nola.* "It's important to respect earned authority because to do otherwise is to deny a specific course of evolution—specifically the sharing of learning for the benefit of all involved. The better we respect earned authority, the better we progress together."

5. *Robert E. Lee.* "Obedience to lawful authority is the foundation of manly character."

6. *Thomas Hobbes.* "It's not wisdom but authority than makes a law."

Chapter 11

Eleventh Doctrine of Gratitude: Show Gratitude to Jehovah God by Forgiving Others

My sweet mother never stopped talking to us children about the importance of forgiving those who hurt us. She believed that not forgiving those who hurt us could easily lead to the disempowering emotion of hate. My sweet mother, however, warned us that forgiveness should not lead to amnesia. When you forgive, stay alert, cautious, and avoid the same circumstances that led to your being hurt. Forgiving those who hurt us, my sweet mother reiterated, is a sign of gratitude to Jehovah God that we are his children and appreciate the gift of life. My sweet mother taught us that thanking God for the experience that led to us being hurt pleases him and makes it easier for him to use our pain for his gain. As Jehovah God in Christ forgave all our sins, we must show to one another kindness, tenderheartedness, and forgiveness (Ephesians 4:32). Jehovah God even begs us to forgive those who have hurt us and to reaffirm our love for them (2 Corinthians 2:5–8).

Even when we are showing gratitude to Jehovah God by bringing him gifts at the altar, he warns that such gifts will not be in good standing if you have a grudge with your brother that has not been resolved (Matthew 5:23-24). But as good as Jehovah God is, he gives us the opportunity to leave our gifts at the altar, go make peace, and forgive our brother before presenting the gifts (Matthew 5:23-24). These Bible verses confirm my sweet mother's belief that gratitude makes many other virtues possible.

What the Bible Says about Showing Gratitude to Jehovah God by Forgiving Others:

1. *Ephesians 4:32.* "Be kind to one another, tender-hearted, forgiving one another, as God in Christ forgave you."

2. *John 20:23.* "If you forgive the sins of any, they are forgiven them. If you withhold forgiveness from any, it is withheld."

3. *Luke 6:37.* "Judge not, and you will not be judged; condemn not, and you will not be condemned; forgive, and you will be forgiven."

4. *Luke 17:3–4.* "If your brother sins, rebuke him, and if he repents, forgive him, and if he sins against

you seven times in the day and turns to you seven times saying 'I repent,' you must forgive him."

5. *Mark 11:25.* "And whenever you stand praying, forgive if you have anything against anyone so that your father also who is in heaven may forgive you your trespasses."

6. *Matthew 6:14.* "For if you forgive others their trespasses, your heavenly father will also forgive you."

Chapter 12

Twelfth Doctrine of Gratitude: Show Gratitude by Reaching Out to Those in Need

My sweet mother preached and lived a life of reaching out to those in need and raised us to do same. She made us to understand that though it's a wonderful thing to thank Jehovah God for the people who make us happy, it is an even greater thing to show gratitude to Jehovah God by reaching out to those who need help. Growing up in a village community and watching my sweet mother and my father reach out to so many people offering their gifts of time, prayer, wisdom, food, shelter, and much more created memories of gratitude that I will cherish forever.

What the Bible Says About Showing Gratitude to Jehovah God By Reaching Out to Those in Need:

1. *Acts 20:35*. "In everything I did, I showed you that by this kind of hard work we must help the weak, re-

membering the words the LORD Jesus himself said: 'It is more blessed to give than to receive.'"

2. *Deuteronomy 15:11.* Jehovah God commands us to reach out to our brother, to the poor, and to the needy in our land.

3. *Hebrews 10:24–25.* "And let us consider how we may spur one another on toward love and good deeds, not giving up meeting together, as some are in the habit of doing, but encouraging one another and all the more as you see the Day approaching."

4. *James 1:27.* "Religion that God our Father accepts as pure and faultless is this: to look after orphans and widows in their distress and to keep oneself from being polluted by the world."

5. *1 John 3:17–18.* "If anyone has material possessions and sees a brother or sister in need but has no pity on them, how can the love of God be in that person? Dear children, let us not love with words or speech but with actions and in truth."

6. *Matthew 5:42.* "Give to him that asketh thee, and from him that would borrow of thee turn not thou away."

7. *Matthew 28:18–20.* "Then Jesus came to them and said, 'All authority in heaven and on earth has been given to me. Therefore, go and make disciples of all nations, baptizing them in the name of the Father and of the Son and of the Holy Spirit, and teaching

them to obey everything I have commanded you. And surely, I am with you always, to the very end of the age.'"

8. *Proverbs 28:27*. "He that giveth to the poor shall not lack: but he that hideth his eyes shall have many a curse."

What Some Great Minds Say about Reaching Out to Those in Need:

1. *Abraham Lincoln.* "To ease another's heartache is to forget one's own."

2. *Albert Einstein.* "Only a life lived for others is a life worthwhile."

3. *Audrey Hepburn.* "As you grow older, you will discover that you have two hands. One for helping yourself and the other for helping others."

4. *Booker T. Washington.* "Those who are happiest are those who do the most for others."

5. *Charles Dickens.* "No one is useless in this world who lightens the burden of another."

6. *Dalai-lama.* "Our prime purpose in this life is to help others, and if you can't help them, at least don't hurt them."

7. *Dana Arcuri.* "Our purpose on earth is to offer a helping hand, compassion, and mercy."

8. *Henry Ford.* "To do more for the world than the world does for you—that is success."

9. *Jesse Jackson.* "Never look down on anyone unless you are helping him up."

10. *John Holmes.* "There is no exercise better for the heart than reaching down and lifting people up."

11. *Leo Buscaglia.* "It's not enough to have lived. We should be determined to live for something. May I suggest that it is creating joy for others, sharing what we have for the betterment of person-kind, bringing hope to the lost and love to the lonely."

12. *Lydia M. Child.* "An effort made for the happiness of others lifts us above ourselves."

13. *Mahatma Gandhi.* "The best way to find yourself is to lose yourself in the service of others."

14. *Muhammed Ali.* "Service to others is the rent you pay for your room here on earth."

15. *Robert Ingersoll.* "We rise by lifting others."

16. *Shannon L. Alder.* "One of the most important things you can do on this earth is to let people know they are not alone."

17. *Winston Churchill.* "We make a living by what we get; we make a life by what we give."

Chapter 13
Thirteenth Doctrine of Gratitude: Include All Things in Your Gratitude

My sweet mother believed and raised us to understand that gratitude is not only for the good things but also the bad. She constantly reminded us that to be the best, we must be able to handle the worst, so we must constantly thank Jehovah God for the dreadful things because dreadful things paved the way for good things to come. Growing up as a little girl that was very fond of her sweet mother, I never stopped wondering why she would pray for everything and everyone including bad neighbors who sometimes even poisoned our dogs and chickens for simply trespassing. When I asked her why she prayed for bad people, her answer was always simply, "In everything give thanks to Jehovah God." I did not really buy this aspect of the doctrine of gratitude until later in life when I was dismissed from school for something that was not my fault. I came home to find my father on his deathbed. I was his only child present when he took his final breath. I will forever cherish those last hours I spent with my father before he went to meet his Maker. Soon after the funeral, the school contacted my mother, and I was admitted back into the school. From then on, I totally embraced the doctrine of gratitude and started including everything in my gratitude—the good, the bad, and the ugly.

Jehovah God's will for us in Christ Jesus is to rejoice always, pray continually, and give thanks in all circumstances (1 Thessalonians 5:16–18).

As Ralph Waldo Emerson once said, "Cultivate the habit of being grateful for every good thing that comes to you, and to give thanks continuously. And because all things have contributed to your advancement, you should include all things in your gratitude."

The memories of my sweet mother's doctrines of gratitude will last in my mind forever, and I will share these doctrines generously with my children and the world as Jehovah God leads me. He wants us to include everything in our gratitude as we embrace the message of Christ, teaching and admonishing one another with all wisdom through psalms, hymns, songs from the Spirit, with **gratitude** in our hearts (Colossians 3:16).

What the Bible Says About Including All Things in Your Gratitude:

1. *Colossians 3:17.* "And in all you do, give thanks to Jehovah God through his son Jesus Christ."

2. *Ephesians 5:18.* "Give thanks to Jehovah God always for all things in the name of our Lord Jesus Christ."

3. *Jonah 2:9.* "But I, with shouts of grateful praise, will sacrifice to you. What I have vowed I will make good. I will say, 'Salvation comes from the LORD.'"

4. *Philippians 4:6–7.* "Do not be anxious about anything, but in every situation, by prayer and petition, with thanksgiving, present your requests to God. And the peace of God, which transcends all understanding, will guard your hearts and your minds in Christ Jesus."

5. *Psalm 100:4.* **"Enter his gates with thanksgiving and his courts with** praise; give thanks to him and **praise** his name."

6. *1 Thessalonians 5:18.* "In everything give thanks, for this is the will of Jehovah God in Christ Jesus concerning you."

Chapter 14

Fourteenth Doctrine of Gratitude: Don't Take Life for Granted; Take Life with Gratitude

My sweet mother lived a life of gratitude and raised us with the notion that we must never take life for granted. She believed and taught us that whatever happens in life happens for a reason and must be noted and appreciated. She always reminded us to pray first thing in the morning as a sign of gratitude to Jehovah God for a new day and a new opportunity. As a little girl growing up, I never could understand why she forced us to make our beds when the bed and covers were so old that the bed actually looked better unmade. I was bold enough one day to think these thoughts aloud. My sweet mother explained to me that if I was not grateful for the old bed and torn bed covers that we had then, Jehovah God would not let me have a bed fit for a princess with new and better bed covers in the future. Out of fear and respect, I reluctantly started feeling grateful for the old bed, torn sheets, and all the other things in my life that I was not too happy about.

The way my sweet mother would talk about living every day as if it was your last since tomorrow is not guaranteed was scary, but it kept us in check and enabled us to live a life of gratitude.

When my sweet mother spent five years with me in the United States, she took in every moment with gratitude. She took nothing for granted, and she shared her doctrines of gratitude generously with all who crossed paths with her.

When I felt the deeper spiritual and emotional need to visit my sweet mother in Cameroon about a month before she passed, I had that thought of not taking life for granted in the back of my mind because I had just recovered from surgery and felt the need to see and feel my sweet mother. Ironically, I met her well, and we spent about twelve days doing fun things together. The day I had to leave for the United States, I promised her I was going to come back in three months to spend more time with her. She raised both hands and, looking up to heaven, responded with, "By the grace of Jehovah God." Not taking life for granted, my sweet mother took out her Rosary, prayed for me, anointed me from my head to my feet, looked me square in the eyes, and said, "My sweet daughter, I love you. Go in the peace of the Lord." If I had known that that afternoon meeting would be the last time I would see my sweet mother, I would have told her more than I did that day. I was taking life for granted. I honestly thought that I would see her in three months.

Jehovah God warns us in Hebrews 13:16 not to take anything for granted. **Gratitude is a virtue that pleases Jehovah God. It is an attitude that comes from the habit of giving thanks. In the Bible, especially in the Book of Psalms, David, who is greatly admired by many including my sweet mother, lived a life of gratitude. Like many of us, David's life was colored with good and tough times, but he never stopped thanking Jehovah God.** As he faced good times and tough times, David always reverted to the truth of Jehovah God's goodness. This attitude of gratitude often carried him through the hardest of situations.

What the Bible Says About Taking Life with Gratitude and Not for Granted:

1. *James 1:17.* "Every good gift and every perfect gift in our lives is from Jehovah God, and cometh down from the Father of lights, with whom is no variableness, neither shadow of turning."

2. *John 3:27.* "To this John replied, 'A person can receive only what is given them from heaven.'" A man can receive nothing—neither office, function, faculty, nor life work, in the kingdom of God—except it has been given him from heaven.

3. *Romans 9:16.* "It does not, therefore, depend on human desire or effort, but on God's mercy."

4. *Psalm 89:20–24.* "I have found David, my servant; with my sacred oil I have anointed him. My hand will sustain him; surely my arm will strengthen him. The enemy will not get the better of him; the wicked will not oppress him. I will crush his foes before him and strike down his adversaries. My faithful love will be with him, and through my name his horn will be exalted." An attitude of thanksgiving can pave the way for any child of God as it did for David.

5. *Psalm 92:14.* With an attitude of gratitude 'they will still bear fruit in old age, they will stay fresh and green."

6. *Psalm 118:23.* "This is the Lord's doing; it is marvelous in our eyes." Everything people admire in our lives is Jehovah God's doing.

7. *Psalm 150:6.* "Let everything that hath breath praise the Lord." The air we breathe has its roots in Jehovah God.

Chapter 15

Fifteenth Doctrine of Gratitude: Show Gratitude to Jehovah God by Choosing Your Friends Wisely

My sweet mother had one person she called her friend. She had wisely chosen this person as a friend when they were young girls. She constantly told us about the love, respect, and loyalty they showered on each other. We grew up watching our Sweet Mother and her friend respect each other's privacy, each other's time, and each other's families. They each had eight kids and spent most of their time nurturing them and being useful members of their village community. My sweet mother always reminded us to choose friends that we could add value to or friends that could add value to us. Like Aristotle, my sweet mother believed and constantly made us to understand that knowing who we are is the foundation of great wisdom and a vital step in choosing our friends wisely. She taught us that choosing friends wisely is a sign of gratitude to Jehovah God and is pleasing to him.

She acknowledged by her words, and occasionally by scolding, that Jehovah God created a world filled with all kinds of people so that we are not limited in our choice of a friend. She warned us that those who cannot choose a good friend amongst the multitude in the universe should be ashamed of themselves. This doctrine of gratitude was a very difficult one for me growing up because as much as I wanted to have wisdom, integrity, and resilience like my sweet mother, I wanted to have many good friends—at least more than one.

I had many friends growing up who I honestly believed added value to me and to the rest of humanity, but my sweet mother thought otherwise—particularly about three of my "good" friends. When I was about twenty years old, I invited one of the three friends my sweet mother was not fond of to a party at our family compound in Akum village. Before I even had the chance to meet and welcome her, my sweet mother had already unwelcomed her and told her to leave and to never come back. She also warned her to leave me alone and look for another friend. When I learned about this frightful incident a few hours later, I was heartbroken. I hid myself in a dark corner and bared my soul to God in desperation. My sweet mother found me in the dark corner, and all she said to me was, "Cry now and thank me later."

When I had my first daughter in Cameroon, I had the honor of having my sweet mother spend one year with me at my Biyemassi apartment in Yaounde, showering her granddaughter with love while continuing to cement her doctrines of gratitude into my thick skull. When she surprised me downstairs one unfortunate evening while I was trying to convince one friend (a friend my sweet mother was not fond of) from coming upstairs where I thought she was with the baby, she gave me the most disappointed look I have ever had.

When I migrated to the United States of America in 2000, I was again blessed to have my sweet mother come and spend five years with me creating memories that my children and I will cherish forever. While living with me, it did not take her long to notice that choosing friends wisely was one doctrine for which she may have to crack open my skull to finally get through. I had one of my "good" friends in another state who happened to be one of the friends my sweet mother had warned me against. I really loved and cherished how much of her time she spent helping me sort out things and talk about events and people. She was usually the first person I talked to on the phone every day and the last person I talked to before I went to bed. She was a link in my daily routine that I could not miss or I would get fussy. If she failed to call me in the morning, I made sure I called her when my sweet mother was not around or when she was distracted by the kids. My sweet mother ignored my defiance for a while, but when I gave birth to my twin boys, she took the perfect opportunity to finally cement this vital doctrine of gratitude into my thick skull. That unfortunate day, I stayed on the phone with this friend for over two hours. My sweet mother lost her cool. She just kept staring at me very disappointed until she finally uttered these unforgettable words: "I really don't know where I have gone wrong with you, but anyone who considers herself a true friend and calls a nursing mother of two newborn babies and keeps her on the phone almost all day gossiping about people is not a keeper. Together, you and your so-called friend will make the world a horrible place."

I spent the rest of this unfortunate day taking care of my babies and listening to my sweet mother's doctrines of gratitude and how I was the only hard-headed child she had. I let my mind wander when suddenly I heard her say, "My friend, are you listening to me? Friendship is not a death sentence. You can have justification for getting stuck with family but never with friends, let alone bad friends. When friendship starts feeling like chains on your ankles, it's past time to let go. Whenever the purpose of friendship as defined by Jehovah God can't be fulfilled, it's time to reexamine yourself, learn some more about who you are, get back to the universe, and look for a wise friend.

And today, after so many years wasted in three bad friendships, all of them my sweet mother had warned me against, I can fully acknowledge that what she could see sitting down I may never be able to see even half of while on the tallest mountain if I don't choose my friends wisely as a sign of gratitude to Jehovah God. In Proverbs 12:26, Jehovah God warns us to choose our friends carefully; if not, bad friends will lead us to sin. Any friend who leads you away from Jehovah God is not a keeper. Consequently, we must ask Jehovah God for wisdom when choosing our friends.

What the Bible Says About Choosing Friends Wisely:

1. *Ecclesiastes 4:9–10.* "Two people are better than one because together they have a good reward for their hard work. If one falls, the other can help his friend get up. But how tragic it is for the one who is all alone when he falls. There is no one to help him get up."

2. *Proverbs 12:26.* "The righteous choose their friends carefully, but the way of the wicked leads them astray."

3. *Proverbs 13:20.* "Walk with the wise and become wise; associate with fools and get in trouble."

4. *Proverbs 17:17.* "A friend is always loyal, and a brother is born to help in time of need."

5. *Proverbs 18:24.* "One who has unreliable friends soon comes to ruin, but there is a friend who sticks closer than a brother."

6. *Proverbs 27:17.* "As iron sharpens iron, so a friend sharpens a friend."

What the Bible Says About Good Friends:

1. *Proverbs 11:14.* "Without wise leadership, a nation is in trouble; but with good counselors there is safety."

2. *Proverbs 27:9.* "Ointments and perfume encourage the heart; likewise, a friend's advice is sweet to the soul."

3. *Proverbs 24:6.* "For through wise counsel you will wage your war, and victory lies in an abundance of advisors."

4. *Proverbs 28:23.* "Whoever rebukes a man will later on find more favor than someone who flatters with his words."

5. *Proverbs 27:5.* "Open criticism is better than hidden love."

6. *Proverbs 27:6.* "You can trust what your friend says, even when it hurts. But your enemies want to hurt you, even when they act nice."

7. *1 Thessalonians 5:11.* "Therefore encourage one another and build each other up as you are already doing."

What the Bible Says About Bad Friends:

1. *1 Corinthians 5:1.* "Now, what I meant was that you should not associate with people who call themselves brothers or sisters in the Christian faith but live in

sexual sin, are greedy, worship false gods, use abusive language, get drunk, or are dishonest. Don't eat with such people."

2. *1 Corinthians 15:33.* "Do not be misled: 'Bad company corrupts good character.'"

3. *Proverbs 16:29.* "A violent person entices their neighbor and leads them down a path that is not good."

4. *Psalm 1:1.* "How blessed is the man who does not walk in the counsel of the wicked, nor stand in the path of sinners, nor sit in the seat of scoffers."

5. *Proverbs 22:24–25.* "Do not be a friend of one who has a bad temper, and never keep company with a hothead, or you will learn his ways and set a trap for yourself."

6. *Psalm 26:4–5.* "I did not sit with liars, and I will not be found among hypocrites. I have hated the mob of evildoers and will not sit with wicked people."

Chapter 16

Sixteenth Doctrine of Gratitude: Show Gratitude to Jehovah God by Using Your Time on Earth Wisely

My sweet mother was such an excellent time manager. She was raised with the understanding that time was one of the most precious gifts from Jehovah, and the only way of showing gratitude to God was by using wisely and productively whatever time Jehovah God blesses us with. My sweet mother believed and preached to us that time management was a very important skill that we all needed to learn and apply in every area of our lives. I can still hear the song she frequently sang about how time waits for no one. She believed that the diligent use of time teaches us the value of life; life, on the other hand, teaches us to use our time effectively.

My sweet mother had no tolerance for anyone who would postpone until tomorrow things that could be done today. She warned against this by constantly reminding us that if anything could be done today then we ought not postpone it, for tomorrow is never guaranteed and comes with its own troubles. She never stopped warning us of the consequences of not using our allotted time on earth wisely and meaningfully. Growing up, I got tired of hearing the following catch phrases:

- Use your time wisely.
- Time waits for no one.
- Time is priceless.
- Time is limited.
- Time flies, and you are the lucky pilot.
- Time is more valuable than money.
- Time lost can never be recovered.
- Don't waste time. Make beneficial use of time.
- Don't give anyone or anything permission to waste your time.
- Time is free but costly.
- You can't own time, but you can spend it.

My sweet mother believed and taught us that if we prioritize, organize, and set goals, we can be better time managers and better ambassadors for Jehovah's kingdom. She valued her time and was very careful not to waste anyone's time for anything that was not meaningful or productive. When I visited her in Cameroon less than two months before she passed, she made every minute I spent with her meaningful and memorable. She told me many stories, gave me plenty of advice, told me how beautiful I was, and most of all how she was so proud of who I turned out to be. She spent the days showering me with the love and attention I so craved. She prayed continuously for the family and for eternal rest with Jehovah God. On the day I was leaving Yaounde for America, I told her I was coming back in two months to spend more time with her. Knowing that time was not guaranteed, she lifted her hands to heaven and looking up to Jehovah God replied, "Only if God permits my daughter." I wish I had known it would be the last time I would touch her or talk to her here on earth! I thank Jehovah God for making it possible for me to spend those precious last moments with my Sweet Mother. That time I spent with her was priceless and so precious.

My sweet mother's life on earth was meaningfully spent. She showed Jehovah God how grateful she was by spending her time on earth wisely. To her family, especially to her children, the gift of her time was one of the best gifts she gave us, and we greatly appreciate it because she gave us something she could never get back. I know that when she got to heaven and gave an account of how she spent her eighty-plus years on earth, Jehovah God was surely happy.

What the Bible Says About Using Time Wisely:

1. *Colossians 4:5.* "Walk in wisdom toward them that are without, redeeming the time."

2. *Ephesians 5:15–16.* "Be very careful, then, how you live—not as unwise but as wise, making the most of every opportunity, because the days are evil."

3. *Ecclesiastes 3:11.* "He has made everything beautiful in its time. He has also set eternity in the human heart; yet no one can fathom what God has done from beginning to end."

4. *Ephesians 5:15–17.* "Be very careful, then, how you live—not as unwise but as wise, making the most of every opportunity, because the days are evil. Therefore, do not be foolish, but understand what the Lord's will is."

5. *James 4:14.* "Why, you do not even know what will happen tomorrow. What is your life? You are a mist that appears for a little while and then vanishes."

6. *Matthew 6:33.* "But seek first the kingdom of God and his righteousness, and all these things will be added to you."

7. *Matthew 24:36.* "But concerning that day and hour no one knows, not even the angels of heaven, nor the Son, but the Father only."

8. *Proverbs 27:1.* "Do not boast about tomorrow, for you do not know what a day may bring."

9. *Psalm 39:4–5.* "Show me, LORD, my life's end and the number of my days; let me know how fleeting my life is. You have made my days a mere handbreadth;

the span of my years is as nothing before you. Everyone is but a breath, even those who seem secure."

10. *Psalm 90:12.* "Teach us to number our days that we may gain a heart of wisdom."

What Some Great Minds Say About Time Management:

1. *Bob Bennett.* "Not managing your time and making excuses are two bad habits. Don't put them both together by claiming you don't have the time."

2. *Bruce Lee.* "If you spend too much time thinking about a thing, you'll never get it done."

3. *Charles Spurgeon.* "Serve God by doing common actions in a heavenly spirit, and then, if your daily calling only leaves you cracks and crevices of time, fill them up with holy service."

4. *David Brainerd.* "Be careful to make a good improvement of precious time."

5. *Rick Warren.* "Time is your most precious gift because you only have a set amount of it."

6. *Robin Sharma.* "Time management is life management."

7. *Stephen Covey.* "Most of us spend too much time on what is urgent and not enough time on what is important."

8. *Thomas Edison.* "Time is really the only capital that any human being has and the only thing he can't afford to lose."

9. *Tom Greening.* "All time management begins with planning."

10. *Victor Hugo.* "He who every morning plans the transaction of the day and follows out that plan carries a thread that will guide him through the maze of the most busy life. But where no plan is laid, where the disposal of time is surrendered merely to the chance of incidence, chaos will soon reign."

Chapter 17

Seventeenth Doctrine of Gratitude: Show Gratitude to Jehovah God by Loving and Accepting Yourself

Loving and accepting yourself was one doctrine of gratitude that my sweet mother exemplified and raised us to embrace without questioning. She taught us to embrace our identity and our purpose by living a life worthy of the calling we received from Jehovah God. She warned us very often that Jehovah God would never help anyone to become someone different from who He, the Lord Almighty, created them to be. Refusing to love and accept yourself is insulting to Jehovah God, who created every single one of us in his image for a purpose. Knowing that Jehovah God loved everyone he created more in a moment than anyone else could love in a lifetime is enough reason to be grateful for who we are and what we are created to accomplish. Growing up as a little girl in Akum Village, there was this song we sang very often. I cannot remember the whole song, but I can never forget the last sentence: "And I just thank you, Father, for making me, me." My sweet mother made us to understand that loving and accepting oneself arms you with self-respect, maturity, godly values, and wisdom to know how to deal with people and situations that threaten your peace of mind. I watched my sweet mother for many years love, accept, and take care of herself as a sign of gratitude to Jehovah God. She believed that loving and accepting yourself was a crucial requirement to loving Jehovah God and loving your neighbor (Matthew 22:39). My sweet mother preached to us that loving and accepting yourself included treating yourself as the temple of God, eating and drinking in a healthy manner, dressing appropriately, exercising regularly, getting enough sleep, speaking positively to yourself, and making wise choices.

What the Bible Says About Loving and Accepting Yourself:

1. *Ephesians 1:4.* "According as he hath chosen us in him before the foundation of the world, that we should be holy and without blame before him in love."

2. *Ephesians 5:29.* "After all, no one ever hated their own body, but they feed and care for their body, just as Christ does the church."

3. *Ephesians 2:10.* "For we are God's handiwork, created in Christ Jesus to do good works, which God prepared in advance for us to do."

4. *Genesis 1*:26. "Then God said, 'Let us make mankind in our image, in our likeness, so that they may rule over the fish in the sea and the birds in the sky, over the livestock and all the wild animals, and over all the creatures that move along the ground.'"

5. *Proverbs 19:8.* "The one who gets wisdom loves life; the one who cherishes understanding will soon prosper."

6. *1 Peter 2:*9. "But you are a chosen people, a royal priesthood, a holy nation, God's special possession, that you may declare the praises of him who called you out of darkness into his wonderful light."

7. *Psalm 139:14.* "I praise you because I am fearfully and wonderfully made; your works are wonderful, I know that full well."

What Some Great Minds Say About Loving and Accepting Yourself:

1. *Amy Leigh Mercree.* "Celebrate who you are in your deepest heart. Love yourself and the world will love you."

2. *Eleanor Roosevelt.* "Friendship with oneself is all important because without it one cannot be friends with anyone else in the world."

3. *Diane Von Furstenberg.* "You're always with yourself, so you might as well enjoy the company."

4. *Heath L. Buckmaster.* "Often, it's not about be-coming a new person, but becoming the person you were meant to be, and already are, but don't know how to be."

5. *Lao Tzu.* "Because one believes in oneself, one doesn't try to convince others. Because one is con-tent with oneself, one doesn't need others' approval. Because one accepts oneself, the whole world ac-cepts him or her."

6. *Mark Twain.* "The worst loneliness is not to be comfortable with yourself."

7. *Marilyn Monroe.* "Wanting to be someone else is a waste of the person you are."

8. *Sharon Salzberg.* "You yourself, as much as any-body in the entire universe, deserve your love and affection."

Chapter 18

Eighteenth Doctrine of Gratitude: Show Gratitude to Jehovah God by Loving Your Neighbor as Yourself

Love your neighbor as yourself is one of those doctrines my mother took very seriously. She was quick to show mercy and to pray for others. We grew up having so many extended family members and total strangers who came to our compound being provided food, shelter, and clothing. My sweet mother was always reaching out to those in need, and even when we barely had enough to eat, she always had something to offer to someone.

As a little girl growing up, I had a tough time embracing this doctrine of gratitude because we had a few neighbors who were impossible to love. Loving them as I love myself, I believed, was simply not possible. Quite frequently, I prayed to God about it. Not getting much closure on this neighbor-loving doctrine, I asked my sweet mother

My Sweet Mother's Doctrines of Gratitude

if not loving these few bad neighbors could cause one to end up in Hell, and she said no. This answer was good but not enough to take care of my neighbor-loving anxiety. My breakthrough came one Sunday afternoon after church when my sweet mother asked me if I listened to the gospel that was preached from the Book of Luke about The Good Samaritan. She reminded me that a neighbor was not only those close to us geographically but anyone in need. She reiterated that whoever we reach out and show mercy to is our neighbor. I was finally happy to know that there were unlimited opportunities to love our neighbors and an unlimited number of neighbors we could love. My sweet mother embraced this doctrine of "loving your neighbor as you love yourself" until her last breath.

What the Bible Says About Loving Your Neighbor as Yourself:

1. *James 2:8.* "If you really keep the royal law found in Scripture, 'Love your neighbor as yourself,' you are doing right."

2. *John 15:12.* "My command is this: 'Love each other as I have loved you.'"

3. *1 John 4:21.* "And he has given us this command: 'Anyone who loves God must also love their brother and sister.'"

86

4. *Leviticus 19:17.* "You shall not hate your fellow countryman in your heart; you may surely reprove your neighbor but shall not incur sin because of him."

5. *Luke 6:27.* "But to you who are listening I say: Love your enemies, do good to those who hate you."

6. *Luke 10:29-37.* "But he wanted to justify himself, so he asked Jesus, 'And who is my neighbor?' In reply Jesus said: 'A man was going down from Jerusalem to Jericho, when he was attacked by robbers. They stripped him of his clothes, beat him and went away, leaving him half dead. A priest happened to be going down the same road, and when he saw the man, he passed by on the other side. So too, a Levite, when he came to the place and saw him, passed by on the other side. But a Samaritan, as he traveled, came where the man was; and when he saw him, he took pity on him. He went to him and bandaged his wounds, pouring on oil and wine. Then he put the man on his own donkey, brought him to an inn and took care of him. The next day he took out two denarii and gave them to the innkeeper. "Look after him," he said, "and when I return, I will reimburse you for any extra expense you may have." 'Which of these three do you think was a neighbor to the man who fell into the hands of robbers?' The expert in the law replied, 'The one who had mercy on him.' Jesus told him, 'Go and do likewise.'"

7. *Mark 12:31.* "The second is this: 'Love your neighbor as yourself.' There is no commandment greater than these."

8. *Matthew 22:36–40.* "'Teacher, which is the greatest commandment in the Law?' Jesus replied: 'Love the LORD your God with all your heart and with all your soul and with all your mind.' This is the first and greatest commandment. And the second is like it: 'Love your neighbor as yourself.' All the Law and the Prophets hang on these two commandments."

9. *Matthew 19:19.* "Honor your father and mother; and you shall love your neighbor as yourself."

10. *Matthew 7:12.* "In everything, therefore, treat people the same way you want them to treat you, for this is the Law and the Prophets."

11. *Romans 13:8–10.* "Let no debt remain outstanding, except the continuing debt to love one another, for whoever loves others has fulfilled the law. The commandments, 'You shall not commit adultery,' 'You shall not murder,' 'You shall not steal,' 'You shall not covet,' and whatever other command there may be, are summed up in this one command: 'Love your neighbor as yourself.' Love does no harm to a neighbor. Therefore, love is the fulfillment of the law."

12. *Romans 15:2.* "Each of us should please our neighbors for their good, to build them up."

What Some Great Minds Say About Loving your Neighbor as Yourself:

1. *Alex Sanchez.* "Pablito, the Bible was meant to be a bridge, not a wedge. It's the greatest love story ever told, about God's enduring and unconditional love for his creation—love beyond all reason. To understand it, you have to read it with love as the standard. Love God. Love your neighbor. Love yourself. Always remember that."

2. *Andrea Bocelli.* "When I get on stage, my first goal is not to show my expertise, but on the contrary, to give a bit of happiness, of joy, of cheerfulness. I am firmly convinced that in order to sing well, you must love your neighbor and be passionate about life."

3. *David Sills.* "When you love the Lord, you long to glorify Him and see the nations fall at His feet in worship. When you love your neighbor as yourself, you share the gospel with him and seek to meet his needs in every way you can, which includes seeing him fall at Jesus' feet in thanksgiving for salvation."

4. *George Herbert.* "Love your neighbor, yet pull not down your hedge."

5. *Girolamo Savonarola.* "Do you wish to be free? Then above all things, love God, love your neighbor, love one another, love the common weal; then you will have true liberty."

6. *Jim Wallis.* "But what does it mean to be on God's side? I believe it starts with focusing on the common good—not just in politics but in all the decisions we make in our personal, family, vocational, financial, communal, and public lives. That old but always new ethic simply says we must care for more than just ourselves or our own group. We must care for our neighbor as well, and for the health of the life we share with one another. It echoes a very basic tenet of Christianity and other faiths—love your neighbor as yourself—still the most transformational ethic in history."

7. *John C. Broger.* "Learning how to love your neighbor requires a willingness to draw on the strength of Jesus Christ as you die to self and live for Him. Living in this manner allows you to practice biblical love for others in spite of adverse circumstances or your feelings to the contrary."

8. *Madonna Ciccone.* "The cross is a very powerful symbol and it symbolizes suffering, but it also is connected to a person who was loving and sharing, and his message was about unconditional love. I tried to take a powerful image and use it to draw attention to a situation that needs attention. For me, we all need to be Jesus in our time. Jesus' message was to love your neighbor as yourself, and these are people in need."

9. *Mother Theresa.* "It is not enough for us to say: I love God, but I do not love my neighbor. St. John says you are a liar if you say you love God and you don't love your neighbor. How can you love God whom you do not see, if you do not love your neighbor whom you see, whom you touch, with whom you live?"

10. *Nicolas Chamfort.* "If you must love your neighbor as yourself, it is at least as fair to love yourself as your neighbor."

11. *Oprah Winfrey.* "Money is worth nothing if it cannot buy you the opportunity to love more."

12. *St. Catherine of Siena.* "You are obliged to love your neighbor as yourself, and loving him, you ought to help him spiritually, with prayer, counseling him with words, and assisting him both spiritually and temporally, according to the need in which he may be, at least with your goodwill if you have nothing else."

13. *Timothy Keller.* "Not everyone is your brother or sister in the faith, but everyone is your neighbor, and you must love your neighbor."

14. *Thomas Jefferson.* "The God who gave us life, gave us liberty at the same time; the hand of force may destroy, but cannot disjoin them . . . Love your neighbor as yourself and your country more than yourself . . . The boisterous sea of liberty is never

without a wave . . . I have sworn upon the altar of God, eternal hostility against every form of tyranny over the mind of man . . . The tree of liberty must be refreshed from time to time with the blood of patriots and tyrants. It is its natural manure."

Chapter 19

Nineteenth Doctrine of Gratitude: Show Gratitude to Jehovah God by Thinking Before Speaking

My sweet mother never allowed any of us to speak without thinking or to voice what is meant to remain a thought only. She always reminded us that even God had to think before speaking into existence the things he created. "In the beginning, God created the heavens and the earth. The earth was without form and void, and darkness was over the face of the deep. And the Spirit of God was hovering over the face of the waters. And God said, 'Let there be light,' and there was light" (Genesis 1:1-4). My sweet mother warned us that though the tongue had no bone, it was powerful enough to break bones if it was used to transmit the wrong words. She raised us to understand that thinking before speaking was pleasing to Jehovah God and goes to show him how much we appreciate the ability to think and speak.

What the Bible Says About Thinking Before Speaking.

1. *Colossians 4:6.* "Let your conversation be always full of grace, seasoned with salt, so that you may know how to answer everyone."

2. *Ecclesiastes 5:2.* "Be not rash with thy mouth and let not thine heart be hasty to utter *any* thing before God: for God *is* in heaven, and thou upon earth: therefore, let thy words be few."

3. *Ephesians 4:29.* "Do not let any unwholesome talk come out of your mouths, but only what is helpful for building others up according to their needs, that it may benefit those who listen."

4. *James 3:5.* "Likewise, the tongue is a small part of the body, but it makes great boasts. Consider what a great forest is set on fire by a small spark."

5. *James 1:19.* "My dear brothers and sisters, take note of this: Everyone should be quick to listen, slow to speak, and slow to become angry."

6. *Mark 15:4–5.* So again, Pilate asked him, 'Aren't you going to answer? See how many things they are accusing you of.' But Jesus still made no reply, and Pilate was amazed."

7. *Proverbs 13:16.* "All who are prudent act with knowledge, but fools expose their folly."

8. *Proverbs 29:20.* "Do you see someone who speaks in haste? There is more hope for a fool than for them."

9. *Proverbs 18:21.* "The tongue has the power of life and death, and those who love it will eat its fruit."

10. *Proverbs 10:21–23.* "The lips of the righteous nourish many, but fools die for lack of sense. The blessing of the LORD brings wealth, without painful toil for it. A fool finds pleasure in wicked schemes, but a person of understanding delights in wisdom."

What Some Great Minds Say About Thinking Before Speaking:

1. *Abraham Lincoln.* "Better to remain silent and be thought a fool than to speak out and remove all doubt."

2. *Alexander Lebed.* "Think before you speak, and don't say everything you think."

3. *Anthony Liccione.* "A fool is made more of a fool when their mouth is more open than their mind."

4. *Benjamin Franklin.* "Remember not only to say the right thing in the right place, but far more difficult still, to leave unsaid the wrong thing at the tempting moment."

5. *Florence Scovel Shinn.* "Your word is your wand. The words you speak create your own destiny."

6. *John Ford.* "You can speak well if your tongue can deliver the message of your heart."

7. *Mahatma Gandhi.* "Speak only if it improves upon the silence."

8. *Napoleon Hill.* "Think twice before you speak, because your words and influence will plant the seed of either success or failure in the mind of another."

Chapter 20

Twentieth Doctrine of Gratitude: Show Gratitude to Jehovah God by Cultivating and Maintaining an Attitude of Gratitude

This is the last but not the least of my sweet mother's doctrines of gratitude. As a matter of fact, this doctrine of gratitude makes most of the other doctrines of gratitude possible. And being in sync with the previous nineteen doctrines will help one to cultivate and maintain an attitude of gratitude.

My sweet mother lived a life of gratitude, and she raised her children always with an attitude of gratitude. She showed Jehovah God gratitude by always being grateful. No matter the difficulties we were going through, she always maintained an attitude of gratitude. She believed that a life of happiness begins and ends with an attitude of gratitude. My sweet mother believed and made us to understand that an attitude of gratitude would confuse the enemy and derail

his plans. Some great ways to cultivate an attitude of gratitude are to write down what you are grateful for, talk about
your gratitude, meditate about your gratitude, express your
gratitude, and seek gratitude (Skip Prichard). The rewards
of practicing gratitude are limitless. People who habitually
practice gratitude by taking time to perceive and ruminate
upon the things they are thankful for experience more positive emotions, feel more alive, sleep better, express more
compassion and kindness and even have stronger immune
systems (Derrick Carpenter).

My sweet mother raised us to understand that having an attitude of gratitude meant we had to create and maintain an
attitude of gratitude always. She believed that if you sow the
seed of gratitude, you will reap the fruits of the Holy Spirit:
love, joy, peace, patience, kindness, goodness, faithfulness,
gentleness, and self-control (Galatians 5:22–23).

Chapter 21
Special Doctrines of Gratitude

When the father of my four adorable children was arrested, detained, and eventually deported back to Cameroon, I hid rock bottom within two years of his departure. My sweet mother was my rock and continued to encourage me day and night to use my rock bottom as a solid foundation for my spiritual growth. Every time I called and poured my heart out she will pray for me but will always end the conversation by telling me this » No matter what happens show gratitude to Jehovah God by not giving up. » Giving up was actually an option that hovered around me quite often when depression crept in and took my suffering to a whole new low level. My sweet mother came up with some new doctrines of gratitude as I battled depression, joblessness, immigration and autism. She will constantly tell me to show gratitude to Jehovah God by starving my fears and feeding my faith. These two additional doctrines of gratitude totally sealed my faith and greatly impacted my spiritual growth and my influence on others.

My sweet mother's Doctrines of Gratitude and my renewed faith in Jehovah God helped in shaping my purpose driven life of gratitude.

I pray and hope these Doctrines will do same to whoever reads them.

May Jehovah God richly bless you all.

It is well.

Chapter 22
Forever Missed: Tributes to My Sweet Mother

A Tribute by Emmerentia Asafor
February 27, 2015

TRIBUTE TO MY SWEET MOTHER- MA PHILO

My sweet Mother, my older Sister, my best friend, in my conversation with you in November 2014, I decided to come to Cameroon to give you a digestive tea you requested , without any second thought.

On my arrival in Cameroon, I met you in Akum on December 27th, where we spent some very beautiful moments. I lay behind you in bed as usual, just like the baby that never grows up as you always referred to me. Little did I know those were my last precious moments with you, Sweet Mummy?

I left for Kumba on December 29th. You and my other siblings were to go back to Yaounde 0n December 31st.On January 1st 2015, the call I got from Mummy Joan that you were in hospital on oxygen is one of those calls no one should have to receive on a day that everyone else is jubilating. My bags had been packed waiting to leave for the US the next day. Sidonie put the bags in the car and we took of immediately for Yaounde. Somewhere along Tiko/ Douala Pa Asafor called me and broke the horrible news. Sido and Ian could not subdue my madness as we diverted the journey to Akum. You arrived the Akum mortuary fresh and plump but breathless, and would not respond to any of the questions Sido, Ian and I asked you. Then, I painfully accepted the harsh verdict of the cold hands of death, and knew it was over. Mummy, although your departure on January 1ˢᵗ prior to my return to the U S on January 2nd was an unimaginable shock, it was equally proof of the love and ties between us. You could not have afforded to sleep away in my absence. Thank you, sweet Mother. I love you Mummy, and my children and I will miss you: the only grandmother they knew.

I pray for grace to do all within my ability to carry on with your very challenging legacy and wish you a smooth transition, until we meet again Sweet Mummy.

Mummy Emmy

A Tribute by Dr. Cornelius Chi Asafor (Pa Ticha) February 27, 2015

Mummy, you will never die. You'll forever live in our hearts every day. Mum, I've always known you to be lovely, caring, warm, happy, inspiring, determined, focused, purposeful, hardworking, disciplined, optimistic, courageous, honest, and generous. Even in the heart of adversity, you remained the same person I knew as a child. You've always prayed for us, and your advice to us was to pray always and lay our hopes and ambitions in the hands of God the Almighty. What all of us have to do now that you have departed from this physical world to join Pa'a Ticha and Atus (we are almost certain) in God's kingdom is to abide by your daily advice and live within the line of your teachings, principles, qualities, and characteristics. Mum, you'll never die; you'll always live in our hearts, walk by our side, and inspire us more than ever before. Your sense of humor will remain indelible in us and continue to help maintain the laughter therapy in our daily journeys. The memories of our lengthy and appeasing discussions by the fireside in your living room or in your bedroom will stay and brighten my days forever. You were our protector and always interceded for us with God. Now that you're closer to him, intercession will be more permanent and the protection more effective and powerful. Mummy, you'll never die. You shall always be present. Mum, your New Year cake, which I brought to you on the thirty-first of December, 2014, is still in your fridge with your heart, a sign of my love to you, drawn on it. That was to have been our last supper, but because of the tiredness you were experiencing, it was postponed—this time forever. Mum, I'm thanking God for your fulfilled life because in our hearts you'll never die. Continue to guide and protect us.

A Tribute by Gisele Chi Asafor
February 27, 2015

You took me by surprise! Barely returned from your stay in Bamenda (Christmas 2014), when I accompanied you to your room, you were sparkling and all smiles. You told me, relaxed as usual, "Did not everything go well and the Lord brought us back?" We had hopes of seeing each other again on the first of January. I did not suspect anything, The Lord decided otherwise. May He take you to His Goodness alongside Pa Asafor and Mummy Imma. Thank you for the love and protection you have always shown to me, especially in my moments of torpor. I am fully aware of the heavy burden that falls on me, with the help of The Most High, I will not disappoint you, Mummy Yooh! Ououhou! Rest in peace.

A Tribute by Florence Asafor
February 27, 2015

Mummy, I have tarried to no avail, and there is no escaping reality. Thank you for those wonderful moments we shared. When I drive home and can't find you at "our corner", I jump on our bed and get a bit of your warm hugs. The day you referred to me as Mummy and asked what my baby had to take for supper, I felt the angels coming to get you, and I could not prevent it. What a courageous mother you were. When you asked me, "Mummy, have I ever complained of pain? Mummy, I am in pain,'" the Lord inspired me to comfort you with music. As smart as you have always been, you asked to brush your teeth when the doctor said I should not give you water. When you asked to take a rest, I did not know it was eternal. My innocent sister stood by me waiting for the miracle, and I hadn't the courage to inform

Mummy Joan that you were gone to be with the Lord. I will keep your wise words close to my heart. Farewell. I know you will greet me with a smile when I am finally home.

A Tribute by Joan Manghe Asafo
March 12, 2015

Sweet Mother, I miss your unadulterated, selfless service, kindness, blessings, love, concern, sense of justice, and the list goes on and on. Love you always.

A Tribute by Joan Manghe Asafo
February 14, 2015

Mummy, it is so difficult and painful for me to talk of you in the past. It was a blessing for us (your children) to have had you as our Mum.

Sweet Mother, what an awesome mother you were—so loving, caring, entertaining, disciplined, kind, God-fearing, peaceful, sweet, and courageous.

Mum, you broke my heart on the first day of January, 2015. And you, shameless death! Why did you snatch our mum from us, leaving me stranded at the CNPS Hospital with the food I prepared for her? Don't you have respect for people? Oh, Sweet Mother, I'll miss your love, your care, your discipline, your prayers, your selfless service, your advice, your sense of justice and above all, your jokes.

Mum, I remember how your prayers and care saved my life in 2005 at the St. Joseph's Hospital in Tampa, Florida, when I had a stillbirth. You always gave me money, clothes, shoes, food, and more even though I am a worker with a salary. Mum, who can do this again for me? Sweet Mother, the vacuum in me is too big. I feel so empty without you, my dear mother.

Sweet Mother, you can never die. I am consoled by the fact that you have joined a new family with God himself as the family head and your daughter and husband by your side. Please pass my regards to Daddy and Immaculate.

I love you, Sweet Mother, and will forever miss you. May you send the heavenly angels to ignite our prayer lives. Mum, you lived a fulfilled and satisfied life. Let your glory be manifested in our lives. Sweet Mother, we count on you to pray us through to salvation and let your hand become a sword to cut down any demonic trees in our lives.

Sweet Mother, I love you.

A Tribute by Joan Manghe
March 12, 2015

Sweet Mother, I miss your unadulterated, selfless service, kindness, blessings, love, concern, and sense of justice. I could go on and on. I love you always.

This Tribute by Evangeline Asafor Ngwashi
January 3, 2015

Sweet Mother, words cannot express the pain in my heart following your very sudden passing into glory on New Year's

Day 2015! You will forever be missed! I cannot thank God enough for blessing us with a mother as God-fearing, wonderful, sweet, hardworking, disciplined, diligent, loving, caring, and kind. You taught us how to pray always, to use prayers as a "steering wheel," and not as a "spare tire." You lived a very active and fulfilled life.

Sweet Mother, you had so much wisdom and humility. Your rise from grass to grace never changed who you were. You raised us to love one another unconditionally and to be one another's keeper, so even in your absence, you will still be present in each of us. You lived by The Golden Rule, treating others as you wanted to be treated! You were salt of the earth and light of the world!

Sweet Mother, your five years' stay in Tampa, Florida, with my children, husband, and me left us with precious memories that we will always cherish! You took care of your grand-children with such love and dedication. I remember our mummy/daughter Monday morning outings at IHOP for breakfast. And what about the visit to Magic Kingdom in Orlando where it took us two hours to locate our car?! Ooh...the memorable road trip from Tampa to Washington, DC?! How can we forget that Sunday in 2004 when we re-dedicated our lives to Christ at the Centre Pointe Community Church? The sky ride at the Busch Gardens? What about the famous "Grandma stew" you cooked with rice? What about that talk you had with your granddaughter about Santa Claus being "an unnecessary distraction" during the Christmas season? Your granddaughter will soon be sixteen years old, and she finally thinks you were right!

Sweet Mother, we cannot forget those agonizing days at the St Joseph's Women Hospital in Tampa, when we did not know if your daughter Joan was going to make it! What about that surprise visit from Pa Asafor?! Five of your children came visiting while you were in Florida! Whoa! They could not bear to see me enjoy all five years alone with you! The rest of your children rang my phone off the hook while you were with me missing their Sweet Mother! I thank God for my wonderful, loving, and caring brothers and sisters! Mummy Flo, you rock!

Sweet Mother, I will forever be grateful to God for making it possible for me to fly over to Yaoundé and spend some quality time with you thirty-four days before your passing; the evening praise and worship time you initiated at Emmanuel's house; the haunting day you, Emmanuel, and I spent on Emmanuel's farm at Ahala; the sweet, fresh corn I harvested, cooked, and we all ate; the chicken Emmanuel got from his poultry, roasted it, and we ate! While Emmanuel and I were busy getting the food ready, you prayed continuously with your Rosary! At the end of our wonderful day together, you raised both hands up, thanked God, and gave him glory! During my brief visit, you gave me your blessings and showered me with so much love and care as you have always done. What about the back rubs after my showers and those moments we spent sitting on the balcony "cracking egussi?!" You told me to be very careful with my ankles because my shoes were too high! You anointed my feet and hands before I left the house for the airport! I wish I had known it would be the last time. This really hurts!

Sweet Mother, you prayed for your last child, Emmanuel, to get married before you die. Not only did he get married before your passing, but he also had a son whom he named Asafor after your husband! When your sight went from bad to worse, you prayed to God for another chance to see before dying. Not only did God restore your sight through a miracle eye surgery, but he allowed you to hold and "see" your last child's son for about four months before your passing!

Sweet Mother, you attended my cousin Nkwenti's wedding and gave him and his new bride your blessing four days before your passing. Your granddaughter, Sidonie, and her husband, Tafor, brought home from Raleigh, North Carolina, your tenth great-grandchild, and you carried and blessed her for a few days before your passing. You spent Christmas of 2014 in Akum village, where you lived for most of your life, surrounded by your children, grandchildren, great-grandchildren, friends, and neighbors, and celebrated the birthday of your last child, Emmanuel, in grand style!

Sweet Mother, one of the last things you asked for minutes before your death was water to brush your teeth. The angels are waiting in heaven to do that for you in heavenly style! You prayed for a quick and painless death, and God granted your wish on the first new day of a new year! May your sweet and gentle soul rest in peace. Tell Daddy and Sister Immaculate (Aunty Atus) that we miss them loads!

Sweet Mother, your seven children, twenty-eight grandchildren, eleven great-grandchildren, your sister, your daughters and sons-in-law, your nieces and nephews, your step-sisters and brothers, your church family in Tampa, friends, and neighbors are left behind to mourn you.

Sweet Mother, I miss you. It will never be the same, but I thank God for your life. Rest in peace. I love you. Always have, always will.

Evangeline Asafor Ngwashi.... "Manghi yoyoyo," as you famously called me!

A Tribute by Evangeline Asafor Ngwashi
January 1, 2015

Sweet Mother, on this, the very first day of January in 2015, my life was changed forever when I got that life-altering call about your passing into glory. It felt like my heart was shattered into tiny pieces. The pain was so deep and strange! I cried and cried and cried! Many assured me that it would get better. Oh, Sweet Mother, how wrong they all were! Some days I feel your absence so overwhelmingly that I simply become delirious! You could never have prepared me enough for this departure! You were too wonderful,

111

courageous, wise, loving, righteous, and kind to be true, yet you were real! I know I must not tie myself to you with tears. I should be happy and grateful that I had all those wonderful years with you. I will allow my grief to be comforted by trust, for I know it is only for a while that we must be apart. I will keep our memories within my heart. I know you are not far away. If I call you, I know you will come. Though I cannot see or touch you, I know you are near, and if I listen with my heart, I will hear you. Your love is all around me, so soft and dear. And then, when I must come that way alone, I will hug you, hold you tight, and with a big smile I will say, "Sweet Mother, I am home!" I will forever miss you till we meet to part no more!

I love you, Sweet Mother. Always have, always will. Manghi yoyoyo

This Tribute by Emmanuel Asafor
February 16, 2015

Mummy, the love you preached is the love you practiced towards all who came your way. The wisdom you portrayed was admired and solicited by all. Your achievements are a marvel even to pessimists. You have written your own history, and you did that in indelible capital letters in the hearts of your loved ones.

I know the glory of your death. The way you left this world is a manifestation of the faith you had in the Lord Almighty. You left in dignity—quietly, uncomplaining, and prayerfully.

112

Unfortunately, I was too naïve and busy (getting more of your medication) to understand that you were leaving.

What a lady you were! What a mum! In the face of the most difficult challenges, you were serene, fearless, and strong-spirited and even encouraged others to be the same. You considered all to be your children, and your sense of sacrifice made me wonder whether you were human. You were a great teacher because the lessons you taught are lessons you lived.

How will I ever forget these last special moments?

- My Christmas 2015 birthday, which you celebrated, offering me a special drink;

- The evening prayers you initiated during the five months you spent taking care of baby Yoni Asafor;

- The blessings you poured on me each time I had to travel;

- The speech you made during my traditional marriage ceremony;

- The quality time you spent with all of us at home and those out of the country;

- Most of all, your unassisted walk from your room through the corridor and into my car on the first day of January, 2015, when we were going to the hospital for the last time.

I feel your absence, and it hurts so. How can it be anything but painful when your phone doesn't ring anymore?

How can it be anything but painful when I don't know where to find you? I am deeply subverted and enfeebled. Sometimes I hear you speaking, but I can't see you.

We, your children, believe in God, the Giver of all life, and that alone comforts us. We know that you are with God and are watching over our every move helping to steer us towards the Lord. We strongly believe.

A Tribute by Asafor Cho, Asafor Cho Ivy, and Asafor Yoni-Emmanuel
February 16, 2015

Mummy, you had an unconditional heart for all and made us to do same. You designed and lived the simplest expression of love and faith, coupled with nobility and greatness which you wore with a lot of humility. You taught us to love God and that all other projects were corollary to this vital dedication. When the lights started glimmering, you told us that your days of old were gone, your mission fulfilled. Tearfully, I say that you are the greatest of mothers, a rose without thorns. Servant of God, fare thee well!

A Tribute by Minette Nupa
January 5, 2015

My beloved grandmother, our rock, our pillar, our fortress, the foundation on which we were all built. You will live in our hearts forever. I will always love you.

This Tribute by Sidonie Nupa Niba
January 8, 2015

I miss you big, Mami. The sound of your voice always brought a smile to my face. You were so strong, grounded, disciplined, and smart and had impeccable memory. I am just so proud to have known you. Thank you for waiting for me to come see you and spend Christmas with you. We will miss you so much.

A tough yet kind lady, a stern yet sweet mother, "Big Mami" was the central force of the Asafor family. She lived a life devoted to God and devoted to serving others. Having lost her husband twenty-six years ago, she remained strong for her kids, grandkids, and great-grandkids. She looked after all and spared none. There is no child in the Asafor lineage that does not have a personal encounter or experience with Ma Philo. She loved with all her heart, and she took care of all those around her, even when they were too grown to need it.

Ma Philo was mother to eight kids: Emmerentia Asafor Nupa, Cornelius Chi Asafor (Pa), Isabella Asafor Epse Fru, Immaculate Asafor (RIP), Florence Asafor Epse Forchu, Joan Asafor Epse Manghe, Evangeline Asafor Epse Ngwashi, and Emmanuel Cho Asafor.

She also leaves behind twenty-seven grandkids whom she touched in a very special way from taking care of them as babies to giving them counsel as adults: Gerald Nupa, Ian-Love Nupa Epse Taba, Minette Nupa Epse Ekosso,

Eleanor Manghe, Desmark Fru, Sidonie Nupa Epse Niba, Nelly Dominique Asafor, Alain Asafor, Gislene Fru, Mafue Forchu, Brice Asafor, Edward Nupa, Faramarz Forchu, Nelly Lum Fru, Hermia Manghe, Manuela Nupa, Ngu Fru, Ndikum Fru, Asafor Fru, Pedro Manghe, Zareen Forchu, Angela Ngwashi, Tiffany Ngwashi, Serina Manghe, Bryan Ngwashi, Ryan Ngwashi, and little Leonie Asafor.

Her great grand babies—Lemar, Leon, Trevor, Manessa, Vanny, Aimee, Nene, Britney, Alex, Ethan, and Daphne—will miss her terribly but are grateful for having been part of her life.

She also leaves behind one sister, Mummy Julia, multiple nieces, nephews, friends, and well-wishers.

Ma Philo's death is a terrible loss to us all. She was such a beautiful soul, and her departure has left big holes in our hearts. We love you, Mom, Sister, Grandmom, Aunt, and Great-Grandmom. May you rest with the angels. You lived a good life, and your legacy will go on forever.

A Tribute by Sidonie Nupa Niba
January 10, 2015

My beautiful, wonderful, and resilient grandmother, you are the only grandparent I ever knew and a sweet, strong force in our family. I thank you for waiting for me to bring Daphne so you could meet her. The videos and pictures put a smile on my face. I thank you for loving me and for teaching me how to farm in Akum and how to be a person

116

of discipline and resolve. I remember my bags of sweet and Irish potatoes you spoiled me with every summer. You will be so greatly missed. Please give my kisses to Pa Nupa, Big Papa, and Aunty Atus. I love you and can't wait to see you again.

A Tribute by Manuela Nupa
January 8, 2015

My dear Big Mami filled with so much energy and enthusiasm, I wish I could see you one more time before your passing. May your gentle soul rest in perfect peace. Big Mami, I really can't quite believe that you've gone until I come back home and see no more of you. I wish I could have seen you before your passing. You were so full of strength and also very disciplined. I remember how well you pronounced my country name, "Nzitai." I will forever miss you. You lived a blessed life. May your gentle soul rest in perfect peace.

This Tribute by Nelly Asafor
January 8, 2015

You were not just our grandmother; you were our mother. It is with tears in my heart that I am writing these few words because it is never easy when you have known someone for years, and in her last days become closer than ever to her, to let her go, forget, or pretend as if nothing happened. What we will always remember is that you were a beautiful,

117

strong, lovely, and hardworking woman. You knew how to welcome your children, and even strangers, with so much care and simplicity. Oh, I remember the fateful day of December 25th in Akum, when I felt you with cold hands and you put them on your jaws and asked Katrine to bring Vaseline for me to rub on them to warm them up. This is an example of your sense of care and concern for those you loved. I can't say anything more than thank you, "Mamman grand-mere." As long as life and memory last, we will remember you. As time goes by, we miss you more—your loving smile, your gentle face. No one can fill your vacant space. May your soul rest in perfect peace, Mummy.

A Tribute by Vanyna and Lizzie Rose
February 16, 2015

We have to pray for our mother, Mama Philomena Mbu Asafor. I know she is with God. We know that. So all I have to say is that she was very wonderful, and that she was a great mother and grandmother. Thank you.

A Tribute by Alain Asafor
January 8, 2015

Death is only painful for those left behind. For those who are moving on, it means freedom. He is like a bird being freed from the cage, this physical body being the cage and the soul being the bird. This knowledge doesn't dull the pain your passing wrought in my heart, but it gives me hope that you are in a better place. Someone told me I could be happy that I have one more guardian angel. You were my guardian angel here on earth, and you will forever be. I have never met another person who prayed for us all. I can only imagine how much stronger those prayers are now that you are back with God. I will miss you! I will miss listening to you sing fine during devotions. I will miss doing your nails and rubbing your feet! I am heartbroken that when I come home, you will not be there to give me a warm hug. All I can do now is thank God you taught us. You gave us the greatest thing any parent can give—that is, the fear of God. What more can we ask? Go well, Mummy, and rest.

Mama Philomena, or as we called her, "Maman grand-mere," was just as much a mummy to us as a grandmummy. She would spoil us with copious meals and all sorts of treats as much as she would scold us for our lazy moments. Two of my most treasured moments with her were the several weeks we spent in Akum in 2007 while I prepared for my GCE and seeing her upon my recent return to Cameroon in 2013. In 2013, I came to see how God had used doctors to restore her sight. There is no greater joy than seeing God's mercy poured upon his children. Oh, how great was my joy. This is what she taught me: "No one can be perfect but God. To become perfect, we ought to let him be our teacher and master." I thank God every day for her life, for all the people he placed on her path, and for her being on their paths and mine.

A Tribute by Brice Atanga Asafor
January 8, 2015

Whatever memory I recall, you seem to have always been there, "Maman grand-mere." I keep in my mind your laughter and your struggle to keep trying to teach me the dialect. I remember how you used to sit on your yellow chair in front of your door, seemingly contemplative over God's blessings for your family. It makes us sad to have to let you go once and for all, and too suddenly. We will walk you along with prayers, that God may keep control of the journey you began. Big Mum, we love you, and we will always remember you as that hardworking, loving mother. Farewell.

A Tribute by Taniform Desmark
February 8, 2015

As we look back over time, we find ourselves remembering all the times you were by us to help and support us. Thank you. Our hearts are still active in sadness, and secret tears still flow. What it means to lose you no one can ever know. But we know. Now you are no more; we will remember all the happy times. Good-bye, Mummy.

A Tribute by Ghislene Akoh, Nelly Lum, Beverly
Neh, Britney Ateh
February 16, 2015

Mummy, shining star of my childhood, Grandma... So the

days I spent with you were the last? So that night Nehneh was playing with you, and you were chatting and laughing with us on the thirty-first was the last time I was to see you? Mummy... Mummy... You didn't say goodbye properly. What will we say to your great-grandchildren? It is well. Oh, the memories live, and we will have you close to our hearts forever! Thanks for your care, your love, and endless presence. Rest in peace.

A Tribute by Mafue Forchu
February 16, 2015

Mummy!!! I am blessed to be able to call you Grandma. You taught me so much!! Even now, I refuse to cry because I feel your spirit with me every day telling me, "You can do it; it's okay!'" You gave us the greatest gifts any parent can give—the fear of God, and love!! We could not have asked for anything better than that. Even now your love continues to pour on your children, grandchildren, and great-grandchildren. Yours was the fulfilled life we all dream of. Thank you for blessing our home and giving us the chance to feel your love and to get to know you. Go in peace as I know you are reunited with your Maker. I love you forever. Mafue

A Tribute by Faramarz Forchu
January 4, 2016

Sweet Mother, Grandma, the last two years you spent with

us, you made an unequaled impact on my life. Every word you uttered and every deed of yours was adorned with such wisdom and grace as to leave me wondering what my life would have been without a grandmother like you. With absolute peculiarity you portrayed faith, selflessness, love, fairness, radiance, and rectitude in your way of life. You were over eighty years old, and despite your health issues, you insisted on visiting me in my tiny room up the hill at Ekounou. Mummy, you alone could think of someone with such affection. I never spent a full weekend in my house because you would call when you didn't see me. I did nothing to deserve such love, and you treated each of your children and grandchildren alike.

I will never stop regretting giving you the usual phone call on that fateful day. I kept waiting to see you in person, and upon arriving the hospital, the gloom surrounding the atmosphere left me weeping. Mama, it was unbearable. Mummy, I promised not to mourn anymore, but even when we pray at home I still weep. Your place in my heart is special.

You nursed a spirit of love in your family, spotless and irreproachable in its very essence, one to be envied by all. Most importantly, you taught us the fear of God and encouraged us to keep singing and praying.

I thank God for the opportunity I had to make you a happy and proud grandma. I will always love you and will keep praying for you till we meet again. God be with you, Mummy.

A Tribute by Faramarz Forchu
September 10, 2016

Missing you, Sweet Mother. We are so proud of you, and we pray that God will give us the strength to walk in your footsteps. Love!

A Tribute by Zareen Forchu
February 16, 2015

Grandma, I am so proud to have had you as a grandmother. I thank God every day for all the time I spent with you. Even in death you manage to spread your love. I miss you more with each day that passes. Your death changed me in some ways, and Almighty God can bear me witness. I cannot be just like you, but Grandma, I will never stop trying. The house will not be the same without you. You live on in my heart. Rest in peace, Grandma. I love you every day. Zaza

A Tribute by Hermia Manghe
April 20, 2018

It has been three years since you left, and I have never found the strength to write a tribute out of fear that I'll never have words enough to describe the void, the emptiness, the vacuum which your passing into glory created within me. I always felt I was going to have enough time to show you how grateful I am and how proud I feel to be your Bébé Awu. I actually feel bad because I didn't get to show you more often how much you meant to me. Regardless of the distance between us, you were ever present in that you never stopped calling me and praying for me. Today I know your prayers for me were not in vain. As a teenager I was naughty in my attitude. You told me, "The patient dog eats the fattest bone." Those have been my watch words since then. I miss you very much, and I hate to think of you in the past tense. Grandma, you are not gone. You are walking with me every step of the way. Your love surrounds me and comforts me in the midst of life's challenges and difficulties. Your prayers and intercession have been the light unto my path for the past three years. The only difference is that I can no longer fondle your braids or massage your feet. But surely you live in my heart forever ♥

A Tribute by Hermia Manghe
February 8, 2015

Grandma, the memory is still fresh in my mind of that glorious day when you left us. That afternoon, the first of January, Mummy Joan and I left Ahala for CNPS to see how you were doing, hoping to see you in a better condition. Little did I know that it was the last moment we had to share with you. You went away as peaceful as the wind. Little Serena Mbu, tired of waiting for us that evening, woke up the next day very anxious as usual only to learn that you were no more. What a shock! Big Mammy, we love you so much, but God loves you even more. That is why he allowed you to go away without suffering.

A Tribute by Angela Ngwashi
February 14, 2015

Dear Grandma, sweet memories fill my mind as I think of you. I remember the warmth of your smile, the comfort in your embrace, and the tenderness in your voice. Not a day goes by without me remembering these things. Even though you are no longer with me, I know that you will always be in my heart. I love and miss you, Grandma.

A Tribute by Angela Ngwashi
January 5, 2016

My dear, sweet grandmother, an entire year has passed since you left us to meet Jesus. I miss you every day, and even though you're not here physically with me, you will always be in my heart and mind.

A Tribute by Alias Muluh, Tanyu Chi Awa on
Behalf of the Family
February 16, 2015

We are grateful to God for the sterling qualities of a golden-laced heart of love and the fear of God which Mami Philo had. Her love for family was so strong. Even after the demise of Pa Asafor, she still held on to the family faithfully in love. Anyi yen shihne'eh Mami. Ala'aneeh Mami. To Pa Asafor and all the children, grandchildren, and great-grandchildren, please remember the words of Psalm 46: "God is our refuge and our strength, a very present help in time of trouble."

A Tribute by Tafor E. Niba
January 10, 2015

Grandma, it was great to see you again only days before the Lord called. Having Christmas lunch with you was an honor. The memories, your positive attitude, your words of wisdom, and your blessing on us and especially on your newest great-grandchild, Daphne, will stay with us forever. I'm sure Daphne would be blessed abundantly having had the opportunity to see you and touch you. May your soul rest in peace! Tafor

A Tribute by Fred Chomilo Ngwashi
January 7, 2015

Sweet Mother, yo yo yo! We love you so dearly, but our heavenly father loves you more. Thank you for your immense work and sacrifice as a mommy, a granny, and a great-granny. Your work on earth is fulfilled, and our heavenly Father has called you to rest by his side. You will be missed in the flesh, but you will live forever in our hearts. Thanks a million.

A Tribute by Nicoline Fru
January 7, 2015

Mummy, words cannot express how I feel. I checked on you the night before you left us and was reassured that you were doing wonderfully. Angels were at work, touching all your loved ones, and I was among them. Mami, you made me plant a seed and then departed so soon. Who is going to enlighten me about the seed we planted? When I was back home, despite your health, you followed me everywhere because you wanted to be with Medzang. You are a loving, caring and adoring mother. We will always love and miss you, Sweet Mother. Rest in peace.

A Tribute by Brigitte Kubri
January 5, 2015

A Godly Mother. Mama Philo is an incredible mother, the epitome of motherhood. And she is a mother who deserves so much more than my meager and insufficient words can offer in this blog.

Mama, your selfless love is irreplaceable, which makes losing you to death an incredibly painful experience. While sons and daughters of all ages carry within their hearts a dull and lasting ache where they once felt love and security, it is important that we all continue searching for the happiness you always desired for us all.

The wisdom writer offers these words in Proverbs 31:28: "Her sons rise up and call her blessed. Her husband also praises her." And so do I. We love you, Mama. Lifted on your birthday says it all; Heaven smiles on you!

This tribute was added by Kennedy Kwende on January 5, 2015:

How sweet a mother you were, always smiling. You treated every kid in the neighborhood as one of yours. If my memories are not failing me, I last met with you here in the US, and that smile and warmth of yours were still the same. Even though we did not cross paths again for a long time, I always remembered the warm treatment you gave me in the early years when I came looking for one of your beautiful girls. Mama, the evenings we all used to share around your fireside putting together the harvest of corn... All I am seeing and remembering is your ever-smiling face and those words of wisdom you always gave me. You were a simple, down-to-earth woman. I know your kids are very proud of you. Thanks, Mama. Adieu.

A Tribute by Lizzie Pamen
January 9, 2015

Aunty Eva and the entire Asafor family, please receive my heartfelt condolences. I pondered on what to say or do that might bring a little bit of comfort to you, but I came back fruitless. However, I know someone bigger than I am who can and will comfort you. His name is Jesus, and He asked me to remind you to lay your burden unto Him, and He will carry it for you. I pray you find comfort in Jesus' words. I pray that Mama Philomena Asafor rests peacefully with Jesus.

A Tribute by Rita Guobadia
January 12, 2015

God called you to glory, and you will surely be missed. A woman with a heart of gold, you treated everyone who came your way as you would treat one of your own. Rest in peace,

Mama, until Resurrection morning, when we will meet to part no more.

A Tribute by Constantine Nadia
March 5, 2015

Mummy, I miss you, especially during my short stay back home when I came to visit you and we embraced each other. I can still feel that love of a mother within me. Why so soon, Mummy? I was speechless; your loss was beyond words. I and Nde miss your funny jokes, Mummy. You were such a great mother. You will live on in our memories forever.

A Tribute by Lum Loveline Wabongwa
March 11, 2015

Mama, you were so knowledgeable. Your legacy will live on forever. May your gentle soul rest in peace.

A Tribute by Marie Pascale Ndikum
March 12, 2015

Mommy Philo, your sudden departure has convinced me that you were truly prepared and ready for the Lord. Painful, but great indeed, because you had a personal encounter with God and waited for his angels. That's why you emphasized to me during my last visit to Cameroon at Pa Asafor's home that you would "never visit us again in America."

Mommy, I miss your sense of humor. I always laugh when I think of you before realizing I am alone. You're gone but not forgotten. May your gentle soul rest in peace. May God console all your children, especially Schwartz, Manyi Eva, and Mommy Emmy and grant them the peace and courage required during this tough time.

A Tribute by Felicitas Atanga
March 23, 2015

To the Asafor boys and girls. You are living proof of the solid upbringing Mama gave you. She will forever live in our hearts. Mama, may your soul rest in perfect peace.

A Tribute by Ivy Asafor Gwanmesia
April 14, 2018

Darling Mummy, I thank the Almighty God for your life. One of the things I admired most was your prayerfulness and strong-minded nature. You equally had a fair sense of judgment. The morning of your death, you repeatedly committed everything about your life into the hands of the Almighty. An epitome of strength I believe you are in heaven. May your gentle soul rest in perfect peace. Your daughter-in-law, Ivy

A Tribute by Dr. Kenneth Che Asongwe
August 2, 2018

Mama Philomena Mbuh Asafor of blessed memories was my auntie whose love and care I was fortunate to enjoy. She protected everyone around her with so much commitment and energy, and my mother (her youngest sibling) was a great beneficiary. I thank you, Mama, for everything you did as you rest perfectly in heaven with the Creator, Our Almighty God.

SPECIAL ACKNOWLEDGMENT

When I think of living a life of gratitude, I cannot help but show my gratitude to Jehovah God by acknowledging my wonderful sister and friend, Rose Ngum Nde Pedjeu, who has been my rock. She met and accepted me when I was at my lowest point in life, and she became more of a sister to me than a friend. Rose is a classic example of someone who would perfectly fit my sweet mother's description of a faithful and true friend. Rose's constant words of encouragement and praise gave me reasons to get out of bed most days. Her wisdom, integrity, selflessness, and generosity were awe-inspiring. She believed in me even in moments when I was so stressed and could easily doubt myself. When I had no one else to turn to during my immigration fight to bring the father of my children back to America, Rose surprised me by accepting to jointly sponsor him with me. My sister Rose guided me and became my pillar of strength when I was at my lowest and even up till this day! With a humble spirit and a grateful heart, I must confess how blessed I am to have such a wonderful lady in my life! I cherish my sister Rose! I pray that Jehovah God will continue to bless and protect my sister Rose and her family all the days of their lives. Amen.

ABOUT THE AUTHOR

Evangeline N. Asafor is originally from Cameroon, near the west coast of Central Africa. As a little girl growing up, Evangeline had a dream of one day becoming an international agent of social change—a dream she thought her native country could not contain. So she migrated to the United States of America in October of 2000. One of her best days in America was the day she was sworn in as a US citizen! She made a promise to herself to be an asset to this great nation, not a liability.

Evangeline has worked as a licensed practical nurse since 2004 in the areas of rehabilitation, hospice, and home health while attending school towards her greater passion of affecting social change as a criminal justice professional. Evangeline loves motherhood, reading, writing, researching and travelling.

 Evangeline's best moments in America happened during her mother's five-year stay with her as she helped with the kids and showered her and her family with unconditional love, doctrines of gratitude, laughter, prayers, tasty cooking, dedication, and memories to name a few. Her stay in

America left Evangeline and her children with precious memories that they will cherish forever.

One of Evangeline's worst moments in America happened when she heard the devastating news of the sudden passing of her sweet mother on the first day of January, 2015. The shock, denial, pain, guilt, anger, bargaining, depression, reflection, loneliness, acceptance, hope, and God's unending presence with memories of her sweet mother's rich doctrines of gratitude prompted the writing of *My Sweet Mother's Doctrines of Gratitude and Her Final Rest with Jehovah God.*

Inspire, Motivate & Equip

To order additional copies of this book call:

214-908-3963

or visit our website at

www.iempublishing.com

If you enjoyed this quality custom-published book,
drop by our website for more books and information.

"Inspiring, Equipping and Motivating Publishing"

50707344R00083

Made in the USA
Columbia, SC
16 February 2019